Trump and the Protestant Reaction to Make America Great Again

Trump and the Protestant Reaction to Make America Great Again explores how polarised interpretations of America's past influence the present and vice versa. A focus on competing Protestant reactions to President Trump's 'Make America Great Again' slogan evidences a fundamental divide over how America should remember historical racism, sexism and exploitation. Additionally, these Protestants disagree over how the past influences present injustice and equality. The 2020 killing of George Floyd forced these rival histories into the open. Rowley proposes that recovering a complex view of the past, confessing the bad and embracing the good, might help Americans have a shared memory that can bridge polarisation and work to secure justice and equality.

An accessible and timely book, this is essential reading for those concerned with the vexed relationship of religion and politics in the United States, including students and scholars in the fields of Protestantism, history, political science, religious studies and sociology.

Matthew Rowley is Honorary Visiting Fellow at the University of Leicester and Research Associate at the Cambridge Institute on Religion & International Studies, UK.

Routledge Focus on Religion

Narratives of Faith from the Haiti Earthquake
Religion, Natural Hazards and Disaster Response
Roger P. Abbott and Robert S. White

The Bible, Social Media and Digital Culture
Peter M. Phillips

Religious Studies and the Goal of Interdisciplinarity
Brent Smith

Visual Thought in Russian Religious Philosophy
Pavel Florensky's Theory of the Icon
Clemena Antonova

American Babylon
Christianity and Democracy Before and After Trump
Philip S. Gorski

Avantgarde Art and Radical Material Theology
A Manifesto
Petra Carlsson Redell

Pandemic, Ecology and Theology
Perspectives on COVID-19
Edited by Alexander J. B. Hampton

Trump and the Protestant Reaction to Make America Great Again
Matthew Rowley

For more information about this series, please visit: www.routledge.com/Routledge-Focus-on-Religion/book-series/RFR

Trump and the Protestant Reaction to Make America Great Again

Matthew Rowley

LONDON AND NEW YORK

First published 2021
by Routledge
2 Park Square, Milton Park, Abingdon, Oxon OX14 4RN

and by Routledge
52 Vanderbilt Avenue, New York, NY 10017

Routledge is an imprint of the Taylor & Francis Group, an informa business

© 2021 Matthew Rowley

The right of Matthew Rowley to be identified as author of this work has been asserted by him in accordance with sections 77 and 78 of the Copyright, Designs and Patents Act 1988.

All rights reserved. No part of this book may be reprinted or reproduced or utilised in any form or by any electronic, mechanical, or other means, now known or hereafter invented, including photocopying and recording, or in any information storage or retrieval system, without permission in writing from the publishers.

Trademark notice: Product or corporate names may be trademarks or registered trademarks, and are used only for identification and explanation without intent to infringe.

British Library Cataloguing-in-Publication Data
A catalogue record for this book is available from the British Library

Library of Congress Cataloging-in-Publication Data
A catalog record for this book has been requested

ISBN: 978-0-367-67684-1 (hbk)
ISBN: 978-1-003-13235-6 (ebk)

Typeset in Times New Roman
by Apex CoVantage, LLC

To Vicki, Alathia, Keira, Tim, Alley, Harley, Maevis and Luna, my quarantine companions.

Contents

1	Introduction: remembering and forgetting the past	1
2	Is MAGA inclusive or exclusive?	13
3	Make America great again	26
4	Make America lament	46
5	Make America better	63
6	Conclusion: confessing history from George Washington to George Floyd	77
	Index	92

1 Introduction: remembering and forgetting the past[1]

> Nor can there be any inconvenience in remembering the mistakes of our ancestors, when all the parties concerned are gone off the stage ... but it may be of some use and benefit to mankind by enabling them to avoid those *rocks* on which their forefathers have split.[2]
> – Daniel Neal, *The history of the Puritans* (1755)

The contest for America's future is a struggle over its past. This book examines the narratives Protestants tell about America's past, present and future. I argue that attitudes towards injustice in the present are linked with narratives about America's past.

American Protestants lack a shared memory. Increased historical reflection, it seems, contributes to polarisation. This book analyses the historical reflection of dozens of Protestant ministers, professors, authors, activists and historians. They approach the past in three ways. Two of them are largely mutually exclusive and contribute to polarisation. Protestants who want to *Make America Great Again* clash with those who want to *Make America Lament*.

This polarisation has many causes and deep historical roots. A third approach to the past might help Americans build a shared memory strong enough to bridge polarisation and support the pursuit of justice and equality. Creating a shared memory will not automatically create a shared politics, but it can help foster more meaningful dialogue across the divide. This third approach, *Make America Better*, is not between the two poles – it moves beyond the *Make America Lament* position. These Protestants deeply and consistently confess historical failures while also recognising how the fight for justice is partly supported by the deeply flawed ideas, persons and institutions of America's past. America's enduring racism and the drive for equality flow from the same source.

Most books about restoring American greatness – many of them linked with Trump's 'Make America Great Again' (MAGA) slogan – mention historical injustice in the national past. Admissions of national guilt may surprise those on the Left. However, the Right's historical criticisms come in very small doses – often only one paragraph. Many Republicans and religious conservatives do not value dwelling on past injustices. However, remembering the good can spark renewal. David Limbaugh expresses this sentiment well: 'Conservatives are not indifferent to America's past sins, but we are proud of America's history and its freedom tradition, which has been a remarkable force for good in the world'.[3] Critics of MAGA decry token confessions, fearing they inoculate against seeing present racism.

This book focuses on remembrances of America's deep history (17th to mid-20th centuries). The Protestant Left and Right look at the mid-20th century as pivotal. For the Right, it was a time of moral definition, American mission and Christian influence. Most Protestants on the Right also take pride in progress towards racial and gender equality. For the Left, this era saw incremental liberation for women and racial, religious and sexual minorities. Many on the Protestant Left also lament declining morality. Right and Left agree the mid-20th century was a point of departure: Is it a departure from historic America or a departure into a more just and equal America?

The debate is not about whether injustice pervades America's deep past. There is surprising agreement on that point. Instead, the debate is over how those injustices continue to influence the present and how Americans should remember or forget ancestral suffering and sin.

Colonial America and contemporary politics

President Trump promised to move the United States towards greater liberty and prosperity. His rallying cry looked backwards. Make America Great Again might be a call to nationalism, but it is also a commission for historians. Perhaps the capstone is the most controversial word, 'Again'. What should be remembered and revived?

Presidential hopefuls often appeal to the Revolutionary era. However, the history of Europeans in North America predates the Revolution by nearly three centuries. The Declaration of Independence was further removed from the explorations of John Cabot (c. 1451–1498) than Donald Trump is removed from the Declaration of Independence. This book analyses how colonial and United States history factor into debates about Trump. What is remembered or forgotten? How are the less flattering parts understood – particularly involvement in racism, sexism, exploitation and intolerance?

The 2020 presidential election occurs one week before the 400th anniversary of the *Mayflower*'s arrival at Cape Cod. The Pilgrims, like the presidential candidates, will be celebrated and confronted, deified and demonised. Competing remembrances will doubtless influence – and be influenced by – the election. Partisans will promote conflicting visions for America and situate the president differently in a grand national narrative.

This book examines Protestant excavations of America's past and surveys how history is used to support or oppose the president's vision to Make America Great Again. It looks at modern remembering and forgetting triggered by MAGA. These historiographic fault lines existed long before Trump. His policies and rhetoric further exposed divisions. Protestant approaches to MAGA spring radially from the slogan – often taking the interpreter to polar opposite conclusions. I will argue for three responses:

1 Make America Great Again
2 Make America Lament
3 Make America Better

All three dwell on America's deep history (17th to mid-20th centuries), but they remember and forget different aspects of it.

For example, the Protestant Left might remember how Puritans were instrumental in the growth of slavery – a fact the Protestant Right might forget. However, the Protestant Left might forget how many Puritan-influenced regions were the first to outlaw slavery once they secured freedom from Britain – a fact some on the Protestant Right remember. There was, it seems, something in the Puritan belief system that facilitated slavery and also led them, earlier than many others, to the conclusion that slavery displeased God.

Patterns of forgetful remembrance were in place long before Trump and reactions to MAGA provide a snapshot into the partisan worldviews of Americans. We gain insights into the hopes and fears of voters, their ideas about good and bad governance, their sense of national pride and shame and their views about the justice of owning historical injustice. Above all, this book explores how Protestants think the past impacts the present, for good or ill.

The colonial past is a foreign country. The Left and Right both vacation there, but they do not like bumping into each other on the beach. A few recent examples illustrate the elasticity of American memory and the love-hate relationship with the past.

Colonial America Leveraged Against the Left: In *It's Dangerous to Believe: Religious Freedom and Its Enemies* (2016), Mary Eberstadt dubs secular progressives as 'neo-puritans' on a 'witch hunt' – irrationally purging America of heresy and impurity.[4] Many denounce the 'Great Awokening' – killing Woke culture with a Puritan stone.[5] Puritanism, in this reading, is a transtheological, transhistorical and transcultural aberration from reason and civility. Similarly, Trump decries witch hunts (an allusion to anti-communist purges or the Salem witch trials of 1692–1693).

Colonial America Adopted by the Right: Debates about America's 'Christian' founding drive proponents into the past. Renewal is often patterned on the covenantal relationship between God and Israel as detailed in Deuteronomy. Some want to Make (colonial) America Great Again. Peter Marshall and David Manuel's *The Light and the Glory* (1973) is the most influential book arguing for a return to America's God. Similar versions of history were adopted and adapted by Moral Majority leaders like Jerry Falwell Sr., D. James Kennedy and Pat Robertson. David Barton carries on this legacy through the WallBuilders organisation. As Timothy S. Goeglein recounts in *American Restoration* (2019), he learned one version of colonial history at church and another at Indiana University. After lengthy research, the church's version was 'closer to the truth'.[6]

Colonial America Leveraged Against the Right: Puritans past star in Kurt Andersen's *Fantasyland: How America Went Haywire, A 500-Year History*.[7] The underbelly of colonial history is leveraged against contemporary prejudice and injustice. Colonial America also inspires fiction. Arthur Miller's 1953 *The Crucible* used Puritans to critique conservative fanaticism. More recently, Margaret Atwood's dystopian *The Handmaid's Tale* (1985) and the sequel, *The Testaments* (2019), were written, respectively, against the backdrop of the Moral Majority and the Trump presidency/#MeToo Movement.

Colonial America Adopted by the Left: Marilynne Robinson, the celebrated novelist and essayist, frequently mines colonial (and Reformation) history in an attempt to challenge conservative Christians to rethink social policy. She puts forward the Puritans as particularly solid foundation stones: 'The American Puritans were the most progressive population on earth through the nineteenth century at least'.[8] Similarly, Stuart Sim, a British academic, argues the Left should adopt a secularised Puritanism and thereby inject a strong dose of moral seriousness into the body politic.[9] An influential fundraising organisation opposing Trump is the Sixteen Thirty Fund which presides over Arabella Advisors.[10] *Arabella* was the ship linked with John Winthrop's famous 'City on a Hill' sermon, and 1630 was the year it sailed. The financial thorn in Trump's side was plucked from a Puritan rosebush.

We should expect complicated interactions with the past since the Pilgrims and Puritans were a variegated, innovative and changing lot. As the historian John Coffey notes,

> Puritanism has been credited (and blamed) for bequeathing a puzzling set of legacies, including the spirit of capitalism, scientific enterprise, Anglo-Saxon sexual repression, companionate marriage, liberal democracy, American exceptionalism and religious bigotry. Puritans

have been hailed as midwives of modernity, and censured as reactionary foes of enlightened values.[11]

New England Pilgrims and Puritans form only a small portion of America's early history. However, they are often the first port of call when discussing national greatness.

MAGA directs attention to national origins. Origin stories are often linked with the present, as historian Abram Van Engen notes:

> The question of American origins, of course, has no real answer. People can argue for their particular choices, but such debates tell us much more about how they view America today than how 'America' actually began. In that sense, historical origin stories function primarily as present-day descriptions.

Van Engen is attentive to what people fail to mention: 'As often as I ask the question [about America's origin], however, no one ever mentions Spanish, French, Dutch, African, or any other national, ethnic, or racial roots'.[12] Most Americans start their narratives with the Pilgrims or Puritans, and, unsurprisingly, they find little agreement there.

Three approaches to MAGA

President Trump possesses 'a Moses touch – an extraordinary talent for planting a stake in the ground and dividing the landscape before him', as Derek Thompson termed his gift in *The Atlantic*.[13] Those who support or criticise him disagree over the meaning of MAGA. Cleavages are messy. For example, the divide is not necessarily between the religious and irreligious, theological conservatives and theological liberals or Republicans and Democrats. The divide is not even between white and minority or female and male. Divergent Protestant responses to MAGA are not easily understood by accounting for power, wealth, ethnicity, theology and even political persuasion.

Trump's slogan cuts between and through groups. Some Protestants are glued together by love for Christ and concern over Trump, as is evidenced by the diverse authors who contributed to *The Spiritual Danger of Donald Trump: 30 Evangelical Christians on Justice, Truth, and Moral Integrity*.[14] Perhaps attitudes towards ongoing systemic racism are the clearest factor that divides and unites.[15]

Chapter 2 argues that Trump's Make America Great *Again* fits into a bipartisan tradition of emphasising national declension. Much of the disagreement about MAGA stems from a central question: For whom will America be great? This chapter explores an inclusive interpretation (Make

America Great Again *for all persons*) and an exclusive interpretation (Make America Great Again *for white Christian males*).

True to its origin in protest, Protestantism remains complex and varied, and responses to MAGA exemplify this. Evangelicalism, though often coded as 'white, religious Republican', is likewise remarkably diverse.[16] About 88% of black Protestants supported Hillary Clinton, and 81% of white evangelicals pulled the lever for Trump.[17]

This book describes three Protestant responses to the president's slogan: (1) Make America Great Again; (2) Make America Lament; (3) Make America Better. A chapter will be devoted to each. These categories relate to views of history, not voting patterns. The two often overlap but are not identical.

The first group mainly comprises conservative Protestants. With notable exceptions, most are white and vote Republican. The second group is populated by both ethnic minorities and whites who likely vote Democratic and are theologically more liberal, again with notable exceptions. The third group is made up of persons who have affinities with both groups, although they tend to lean towards the *Make America Lament* position. They aim to communicate across the divide and call for a nuanced understanding of the good and bad in American history.

Chapter 3 begins by exploring the burden of memory that *Make America Great Again* Protestants carry around. They primarily feel burdened by court cases that, from their perspective, took America away from its Christian foundation. I explore the interpretation of the past by several Protestant authors: Robert Jeffress, Cal Thomas, Os Guinness, Eric Metaxas, Michael L. Brown and a cadre of prophets or 'prophecy experts'. These authors differ in their approach to MAGA, but they agree that the renewal of American greatness requires a return to God. Returning to God necessitates a recovery of what made America great between 1620 and the 1950s.

Make America Great Again Protestants feel like MAGA haters repudiate the national past. They think the Left disrespects history, disregards legal documents and mocks American ideals – castigating the founders as hypocritical at best and evil at worst. These Protestants are aware of national sins, but many see little use in dwelling upon them. They are aware of racists on the Right, but they think racists also congregate on the Left. Of particular importance, they think Democrats target minorities through abortion – what many consider to be a new slavery or new eugenics. Their decline narrative begins in the 1950s, and the solution to problems lies in looking to the future while glancing fondly at the past. They consider the Left to be iconoclasts – running through the national past and smashing anything impure. Many *Make America Great Again* Protestants seem only dimly aware that the Protestant Left even exists.

In Chapter 4, I describe *Make America Lament* Protestants who carry around a very different burden of memories. Many lament the declining Christian influence. However, they are more concerned with remembering the theft of land from American Indians, the accumulation of wealth on the backs of African Americans and the marginalisation of women throughout history. The past, they argue, is not in the past – citing ongoing prejudice in forms that range from voter suppression to the New Jim Crow to police brutality. I describe the contours of historical remembrance by examining several Protestant authors: Sheri Faye Rosendahl, Cornel West, Michael Eric Dyson, Jemar Tisby, Jonathan Walton, Jonathan Wilson-Hartgrove, Mark Charles and Soong-Chan Rah. When they hear 'Make America Great Again', they argue that the nation's history should prompt lament.

Make America Lament Protestants feel that MAGA denies, dismisses or glorifies America's oppressive, racist, sexist, land-grabbing past. Worse yet, many believe MAGA is a call to restore some of these unsavoury features. These Protestants can tell stories of progress, but the present political situation has made declension narratives more poignant. Solutions to present problems often involve confronting the past, but America should be open to new possibilities and seek the input of those historically marginalised from power. Of course, they also want to make America *better* (see the following discussion), but they do so by emphasising past injury and inequity. Although they may admire much in the American past, they seem to worry that patriotic appeals might short-circuit repentance and restitution. Many on this side consider MAGA Protestants to be idolaters – genuflecting before the gods of affluence and white supremacy. They often describe the Protestant Right as un-Christian.

A final group is discussed in Chapter 5. *Make America Better* Protestants do not shy away from America's unrighteous moments, and they insist on remembering them often. However, they also appeal to the high ideals of the American founding and argue that criticism is patriotic. They frequently speak of two Americas – the reality and the ideal. The reality was unequal and unjust; the ideal was inspiring and laid the groundwork for equality. I survey the works of David N. Moore, Van Jones, Jim Wallis, Eric Mason, John Fea and Marilynne Robinson. These authors embrace American history – the good and the bad. A better America comes through lament, but Americans should also be energised by looking at who and what made America progressively better. Persons in this camp are often partisans but charitable partisans calling everyone to Make America *Better*.

A concluding chapter argues for the urgency of historical reflection. After the killing of George Floyd by a Minneapolis police officer in May 2020, competing versions of American history have been on full display. In his July 2020 speech before Mount Rushmore, President Trump delivered what was perhaps his clearest articulation of when America was great and who made it great. This speech is contrasted with Al Sharpton's eulogy for George Floyd and his subsequent speech at a Juneteenth rally in Tulsa. Sharpton argues that Trump's version of American history must be laid to rest before the nation can progress towards true greatness.

The conclusion then reflects on the three approaches to the past. When Protestants hear MAGA, they want to discuss America's deep past (17th c. to mid-1950s). However, they remember and forget different things. If we desire to bridge polarisation in the present, Americans need more of a shared memory. If *Make America Great Again* Protestants have a hard time articulating what went wrong in American history, *Make America Lament* Protestants have a hard time articulating what went right. The *Make America Better* approach seems most likely to foster a shared understanding of the past that can bridge political divides and move the nation towards justice and equality.

Can national greatness be measured?

Much of the debate that unfolds in this book is over how to weigh the nation. Many on the Right and the Left have their own systems of weights and measures. Unsurprisingly, they reach different conclusions. There are many difficulties associated with placing America in the scales, and the rest of the book will explore how individual Protestants navigate these questions.

What calculus would one use to measure the greatness of a nation? Do we compare historical America to beliefs and practices in other nations at the time? Is the country to be measured against its own ideals? Do we measure a historical era by how far it progresses towards our standards or by how far it still falls short? Do we compare historical America to beliefs and practices in modern America or in other nations?

The problem of standards is acute, but there is also the issue of assigning weights to events, actions, beliefs and attitudes. In the scales of justice, does the democratic impulses of the Puritans counterbalance the participation in expelling American Indians? How does Thomas Jefferson's defence of liberty weigh against the exclusion of women from power? How much is George Washington credited for his leadership, and how much is he debited for slavery? Should Abraham Lincoln be revered for emancipating slaves or reviled because he did not think they should be equal with whites? Is Margaret Sanger a hero because she fought for freedom for vulnerable women, or is she a racist because of her support for eugenics?

Protestants would answer these questions differently. Some might condemn Sanger's white supremacy as they overlook Abraham Lincoln's. Others might wink at Sanger's racism while critiquing Lincoln's. Still others might condemn both or overlook the failings of both.

Although the attempt to weigh the relative goodness of a nation is fraught with difficulties, it is valuable to wrestle with these questions. They help people engage meaningfully with complexities and contradictions in America's chequered past.

A note on method

For this study, I have not waded deeply into social media, talk radio or the blogosphere – places where historians fear to tread.[18] I have primarily restricted myself to published books by Protestant ministers, professors, authors, activists and historians. I have taken a broad definition of both 'Protestant' and what I consider 'historical reflection'. In mainly restricting myself to persons who published books, I have given less attention to sermons or to Protestants in the pews. I focus on Protestants because they greatly influence American politics and because this book grew out of a project on Protestant Political Thought at the Cambridge Institute on Religion & International Studies (Clare College, University of Cambridge). Doubtless, a wider scope would have added richly to the picture painted here.

Within each political party, there is a bewildering mixture of values, temperaments, beliefs, motivations and experiences. I have tried to emphasise diversity within each group as I reconstruct beliefs.

In the wake of Trump's election, a wave of books tried diagnosing the cause of national schisms. Consider a recent book by Arthur C. Brooks, a centre-Right Catholic, President of the American Enterprise Institute and faculty member at the Harvard Kennedy School and Harvard Business School. He is one of many trying to reach across the divide. The fundamental problem in American politics is that 'We are living in a culture of contempt'.[19] Contempt is worse than hatred. It uses everything negative in an opponent as grounds for hatred, and it twists everything positive into a weapon. Everything confirms competing and incompatible beliefs in righteousness.[20] In response to contempt, there are often three options: '(1) ignore, (2) insult, or (3) destroy'.[21] His book advocated love as a viable fourth response. His position is similar to Van Jones who argued in *Beyond the Messy Truth* that the country suffers from a 'dysfunctional "politics of accusation"' that needs to be replaced with 'a "politics of confession"'.[22]

Bryan Loritts, a prominent African American pastor of a multicultural congregation, offers another diagnosis. Many white evangelicals lack *sympathy*. Erroneous beliefs, assumptions and practices led them to support Trump, 'but it was only when I traced the proverbial crayon across them that a picture emerged for what I was really feeling and sensing – a lack of sympathy'.[23] This deficit of sympathy was all the more pronounced since the nation transitioned from a president who could sympathise with black and brown Americans to a president who was sympathetically anaemic. When headlines of police brutality break, 'White evangelicals seem to have earned a PhD in statistics, but they're at a third-grade level when it comes to sympathy'.[24] Loritts argues that this lack of sympathy has deep historical roots, and his book aims to bridge the divide forged by centuries of injustice.

In *Stranger in Their Own Land*, the sociologist Arlie Russell Hochschild argues for the construction of 'an empathy bridge'. Empathy is denigrated because it is misunderstood. It is taken as synonymous with 'agreement' or 'consent'. Again Hochschild: 'We, on both sides, wrongly imagine that empathy with the "other" side brings an end to clearheaded analysis when, in truth, it's on the other side of that bridge that the most important analysis can begin'.[25]

If Americans are serious in their conviction that political opponents are dangerous, they should avoid confirming the prejudice of rivals. Christian Picciolini, a former white supremacist leader who works to deradicalise individuals of many political and religious persuasions, recently argued that the tactics in use by many in our outrage culture are counterproductive. He understands 'the negative implications of such dehumanizing tactics' and labours to earn 'trust' and 'listen with empathy' as he seeks to hold people accountable for their beliefs and actions. He believes 'the only way to break this [nation-wide] cycle of hate we are stuck in is to not distance ourselves from the problem, but to invest in one another, and in our failing "human infrastructure"'.[26]

The empathetic approach I endeavour to apply need not conclude that there are 'very fine people' on both sides of every conflict. Rather, it affirms that people on both sides think they have very fine reasons for their beliefs and actions. If empathy sharpens critique, our public 'discourse' might be worthy of that name.

Notes

1. I would like to thank participants in conferences at Cambridge and Duke who provided valuable feedback. I am also indebted to the anonymous reviewers and to Rebecca Shillabeer, Amy Doffegnies and Christopher Mathews who helped this project through to production.
2. Daniel Neal, *The History of the Puritans, or, Protestant Non-conformists, . . . with an Account of Their Principles* (Dublin, 1755) II:viii.
3. David Limbaugh, *Guilty by Reason of Insanity: Why the Democrats Must Not Win* (Washington, DC: Regnery, 2019), 8.
4. Mary Eberstadt, *It's Dangerous to Believe: Religious Freedom and Its Enemies* (New York: HarperCollins, 2016).
5. For example, Jason M. Morgan, 'The Great Awokening: The Puritan Roots of the Social Justice Warrior', *The New Oxford Review* (Jan – Feb 2019). Online: -the-social-justice-warrior/. Retrieved 4 Mar 2020; P. J. O'Rourke, 'Puritanism Is Back . . . and Welcome to It: Martyrdom Has Become "Inclusive"',

Introduction   11

The Spectator (9 Oct 2019). Online: https://spectator.us/puritanism-back-welcome/. Retrieved 4 Mar 2020; Bo Winegard and Ben Winegard, 'The Preachers of the Great Awokening', *Quilette* (21 Sept 2018). Online: https://quillette.com/2018/09/21/the-preachers-of-the-great-awokening/. Retrieved 4 Mar 2020.

6   Timothy S. Goeglein and Craig Osten, *American Restoration: How Faith, Family, and Personal Sacrifice Can Heal Our Nation* (Washington, DC: Regnery, 2019). He cites, as the incorrect version, Howard Zinn's *A People's History of the United States, 1492–Present* (New York: Harper & Row, 1980). A popular rebuttal to Zinn is Larry Schweikart and Michael Allen's *A Patriot's History of the United States: From Columbus's Great Discovery to the War on Terror* (New York: Sentinel, 2004). Also notable are two works by the Jewish radio host Michael Medved, *The American Miracle: Divine Providence in the Rise of the Republic* (New York: Crown, 2016); idem., *God's Hand on America: Divine Providence in the Modern Era* (New York: Crown, 2019).

7   Kurt Andersen, *Fantasyland: How America Went Haywire, A 500-Year History* (New York: Random House, 2017).

8   Marilynne Robinson, *What Are We Doing Here?* (New York: Farrar, Straus and Giroux, 2019), 61.

9   Stuart Sim, *Twenty-First Century Puritanism: Why We Need It and How It Can Help Us* (Champaign: Common Ground, 2018).

10 By Scott Bland and Maggie Severns, 'Documents Reveal Massive "Dark-money" Group Boosted Democrats in 2018', *Politico* (19 Nov 2019). Online: www.politico.com/news/2019/11/19/dark-money-democrats-midterm-071725. Retrieved 12 Feb 2020.

11 John Coffey, 'Puritan Legacies', in John Coffey and Paul C. H. Lim (eds.), *The Cambridge Companion to Puritanism* (Cambridge: Cambridge University Press, 2008), 327–45 (327).

12 Abram C. Van Engen, *City on a Hill: A History of American Exceptionalism* (New Haven: Yale University Press, 2020), 1–2.

13 Derek Thompson, 'Donald Trump's Language Is Reshaping American Politics', *Atlantic* (15 Feb 2018). Online: www.theatlantic.com/politics/archive/2018/02/donald-trumps-language-is-reshaping-american-politics/553349/. Retrieved 25 Apr 2020.

14 Ronald J. Sider (ed.), *The Spiritual Danger of Donald Trump: 30 Evangelical Christians on Justice, Truth, and Moral Integrity* (Eugene: Cascade, 2020).

15 Among Never Trumpers, racism was an important factor (Robert P. Saldin, *Never Trump: The Revolt of the Conservatives* [Oxford: Oxford University Press, 2020], 184–94).

16 Thomas S. Kidd, *Who Is an Evangelical? The History of a Movement in Crisis* (New Haven: Yale University Press, 2019), 154; cf. Angela Denker, *Red State Christians: Understanding the Voters Who Elected Donald Trump* (Minneapolis: Fortress Press, 2019), 286.

17 Kidd, *Who Is an Evangelical?*, 145.

18 The online life of MAGA requires a history of its own. See examples in Paul Booth, Amber Davisson, Aaron Hess, and Ashley Hinck, *Poaching Politics: Online Communication in the 2016 Presidential Election* (New York: Peter Lang, 2018), 42, 101, 111–12, 137, 147, 155.

19 Arthur C. Brooks, *Love Your Enemies: How Decent People Can Save America from the Culture of Contempt* (New York: Broadside, 2019), 5.

20 On the self-confirming nature of modern politics, see Jonathan Haidt, *The Righteous Mind: Why Good People Are Divided by Politics and Religion* (London: Penguin, 2012).

21 Brooks, *Love Your Enemies*, 33.
22 Van Jones, *Beyond the Messy Truth: How We Came Apart, How We Come Together* (New York: Ballantine, 2017), xv.
23 Bryan Loritts. *Insider Outsider: My Journey as a Stranger in White Evangelicalism and My Hope for Us All* (Grand Rapids: Zondervan, 2018), 143.
24 Ibid., 144.
25 Arlie Russell Hochschild, *Strangers in Their Own Land: Anger and Mourning on the American Right* (New York: New Press, 2016), xi.
26 Christian Picciolini, *Breaking Hate: Confronting the New Culture of Extremism* (New York: Hachette, 2020), xxxiv, xxiii.

2 Is MAGA inclusive or exclusive?

The rise and fall of America

Whether or not America was founded as a Christian nation, it was certainly founded on fears of decline. Many colonists feared that the spiritual declension in Old England would soon manifest itself in New England. As one poignant example, the Massachusetts Historical Society holds a poem by Thomas Tillam, 'Uppon the first sight of New-England' (29 June 1638).[1] It begins by hailing this 'holy-land' and ends anxiously musing over the possibility of judgement – and Tillam's feet had not even hit dry ground! The prospect of divine terror and the promise of divine blessing were twin themes that ran throughout colonial history. The dialectic proved fruitful for these hopeful and humbled people.

In sermons and print, colonial ministers warned of imminent divine judgement because of covenant unfaithfulness. This 'Jeremiad' tradition aimed to forestall decline with renewed godliness.[2] Americans still rehearse narratives of progress and decline, especially when they argue about politics. For example, Chris Hedges's *America: The Farewell Tour* (Christian Left) can be contrasted with Michael L. Brown, *Saving a Sick America* (Christian Right).[3] The authors disagree over how to interpret history, where to lay blame and how to heal America, but the similarities are as striking as the differences. Among both major parties, there is a widespread view that America is in decline – and both Hedges and Brown supported populists like Bernie Sanders and Donald Trump.

As Robert P. Jones details in *The End of White Christian America*, 53% of Americans believe in cultural decline. The difference is pronounced when race and religion are accounted for: 43% of black Protestants, 58% of white mainline Protestants and 72% of white evangelical Protestants say that American culture has 'mostly changed for the worse' since the 1950s.[4]

Along with narratives of decline, Americans consume stories of victimisation. If one wants real-life stories of those hurt (and killed) by progressive policies, they can open Kayleigh McEnany's *The New American Revolution* (Christian Right).[5] If one wants real-life stories of how the culture wars for 'biblical' and 'traditional' values hurt other Americans, they can pick up Jonathan Wilson-Hartgrove's *Revolution of Values* (Christian Left).[6] Noting the fact that both sides keep track of the mounting body count, of course, does not imply moral equivalency. That is another discussion entirely. I simply raise a cautionary flag over the leap from sensed victimisation (or identification with a victim) to the conclusion that one's policies are entirely righteous.

Most humans find it hard to imagine that people on both sides of a conflict – for different reasons and to differing degrees – feel victimised. It is even harder to think that those defending victims might also be perpetrators. Most think of victimisation in a zero-sum, winner-takes-all fashion. Acknowledging any injury done to an opponent, they think, means undermining the war effort (at best) or conceding the entire war (at worst). Self-criticism becomes self-defeating. There follows a Manichaean struggle to the death over who is the true victim. The pure victim then vanquishes the 'other' and discredits the deceased's claims to victimhood.[7]

Donald Trump's *Crippled America: How to Make America Great Again* (2015) fits into a long tradition of political and religious argumentation about victimisation and decline.[8] He positions himself as a populist outsider defending the ordinary person from hostile elites. According to Yale sociologist Philip Gorski,

> Right-wing populism is a political ideology that pits the common people against a corrupt elite that has allied itself with an undeserving other, and the leader as a man of the people and the scourge of the elites who will defend the people and expel the invading other.[9]

Trump is clear about who the victims are and why perpetrators act as they do. But when was America great? What made it great? And for whom was America great? On these points, Trump is usually vague. His book switches rapidly between greatness and declension (it was the best of times; it was the worst of times) – a dialectic presidential hopefuls try to exploit. Whether he knew it or not, Trump also tapped into centuries of Protestant narratives about victimisation and decline – but he did so with the optimism of one steeped in Norman Vincent Peale's gospel.

Discussion of MAGA invariably leads to debates about history. History is a common ground, and for that reason, it is also a battleground. In short, modern Americans fight a proxy war in America's past. Protestants do not approach history with shared assumptions and experiences. As a foretaste of what is to come, consider a response to the 2016 election by Mark Charles (a Navajo minister, activist and 2020 Independent presidential candidate) and Soong-Chan Rah (a Korean-born American and seminary professor):

> The myth of American exceptionalism is a bipartisan and unifying theme for most every American. . . . After her win in the South Carolina primary, Hillary Clinton responded to the Trump Campaign slogan 'Make America Great Again' by telling the cheering Democratic audience that 'America never stopped being great'. . . . In the 2016 presidential campaign the candidate from the Grand Old Party was a white land-owning male who was campaigning to make America explicitly white supremacist, racist, and sexist again. The Democratic candidate was a white woman who was pleading for the opportunity to help keep our nation's white supremacy and racism implicit.[10]

Clinton wanted to 'Keep America Great' – ironically Trump's 2020 slogan before he adopted 'Transitioning to Greatness'. As this commentary by Charles and Rah demonstrates, claims about American greatness prompt minority reports.

In the run-up to the 2016 election, *The New York Times* asked readers 'When Was America Greatest?' The Trump campaign did not respond. Pollsters found that Trump supporters chose 'the year 2000. But 1955, 1960, 1970 and 1985 were also popular'. Democrats 'were more likely to pick a year in the 1990s, or since 2000. After 2000, their second-most-popular answer was 2016'. Most Democrats and Republicans chose 2000 as America's greatest year. Democrats remembered Bill Clinton's last year, Republicans anticipated George W. Bush's inauguration, and both remembered a world before terrorism altered the New York City skyline.[11] Most of those supporting MAGA, it seems, have a taste for the vintage rather than the antique.

On the surface, this *New York Times* article seems to present a problem for this current study. If 2000 was the greatest for all, if Republican nostalgia extends only to the 1950s, and if Democrats were pretty happy with the Clinton and Obama years, then why focus on America's deep history (17th to mid-20th centuries)? MAGA directly appeals to the good old days. But 'The old days had their own old days', as James Poniewozik notes.[12] Both the 'old' old and 'new' old days impact perceptions of the present.

Trump's words, actions and motivations

Those who love or loathe the president expend enormous energy analysing his words, actions and motivations. These analyses often speak volumes about the values of the one interpreting him. In the words of Michael D'Antonio's pre-election biography, 'Trump was a walking inkblot test'.[13]

It can be notoriously difficult to understand what he means. 'Untangling any single Trump claim', D'Antonio asserts, 'requires great effort and generally yields little of value'.[14]

In *The Art of the Deal* (1987), Trump said he communicates via 'truthful hyperbole'.[15] The president also has bouts of lucid brevity, as when he said in *The America We Deserve* (2000): 'I'm not a professional historian, let alone a distinguished historian. I'm a guy who knows how to put big deals together'.[16] Statistical analysis shows that Trump, when compared to other candidates and presidents, rarely mentions history.[17] Americans elected a businessman, and they debate his version of history.

Heat-filled analysis of his words does not necessarily produce more light. Words can reveal or conceal. Actions may speak louder than words, and most observers cannot agree on how to interpret actions. Motivations are notoriously hard to pin down. Caution, nuance and humility should temper analysis, but these virtues are often targeted first in partisan conflicts precisely because caution does not help the war effort.

Consider the difficulty in interpreting words: It can be hard to distinguish one president's official statements from another, as the decontextualised examples illustrate:

- Today, we are here to honor the extraordinary contributions of African Americans to every aspect of American life, history, and culture. From the earliest days of this nation, African American leaders, pioneers, and visionaries have uplifted and inspired our country in art, in science, literature, law, film, politics, business, and every arena of national life. The depth and glory of these contributions are beyond measure.
- In every moment of our history, African Americans have called our nation to greatness.
- The laws . . . harmed African American communities, and far, far greater than anybody else.
- Today, we remember the heroic legacy of African Americans who bravely battled oppression to usher in a bright new dawn of freedom.
- So we pledge, in the honor of our great African American community, to build a future when every American child can live in safety, dignity, liberty, and peace. As Americans, we all share the same dreams, the same hopes, and the same magnificent destiny. We are now, and will forever be, one people, one family, and one glorious nation under God.

These statements were all from President Trump, and all from one speech.[18]

Historians sometimes have to assess an individual based on one record. Nothing else survived. If this speech were our only window into Trump's mind, it appears he believes African Americans were historically wronged, that they are still discriminated against, that they were part of what made America great and they are essential to restoring greatness.

Those desiring to acquit the president of racism need look no further. His supporters are often aware of (and embarrassed by) contrary evidence – they need not consult his fossilised tirades on Twitter. However, supporters think speeches like the one cited here reveal the true Trump. In the words of Roderick P. Hart, 'They are willing to work through Trump's words to find his true intentions'.[19] Supporters might overlook his offensive words and focus on outcomes – particularly the economic benefits of his pre-COVID-19 economy. They also note high-profile minorities who have shown support, like Kanye West or Candace Owens.

Consider Ralph Reed's recent assessment of Trump's actions (particularly those benefiting minorities):

> Trump's media critics parse his tweets like they are studying the Holy Writ and roam the world for his tax returns as though in search of the Holy Grail. Meanwhile, they ignore his works, deeds, and amazing accomplishments. . . . Trump sometimes says (or tweets) things I wish he wouldn't.[20]

For critics, Trump's words are bad, and his actions are worse. For the faithful, his words are questionable, but his actions are beneficial.

For many Protestants, the diverse group of ministers who support the president cast doubt on his racism.[21] As Sarah Posner comments in *Unholy*, many religious rallies supporting Trump are very diverse, 'crushing the impression created by Trump's nearly all-white MAGA rallies'.[22] Trump's spiritual advisor, Paula White-Cain, said that Trump is 'absolutely not a racist' and treats 'all people' equally. Accusations of racism – invented after Trump ran for president – come from the 'pit of hell'.[23]

In the words of Stephen E. Strang, another religious leader who supports Trump despite flaws, 'Nothing like this has ever happened. Trump's supporters were from every race, creed, and socioeconomic background'.[24] This diversity was evidenced by those laying hands on the president before his speech to the 'Evangelicals for Trump' rally at El Rey Jesus Church in Miami (January 2020). If diversity is the yardstick of truth, Trump's evangelical supporters think they measure up.

As will be discussed in detail later, others sharply disagree. They remind people of Trump's slurs and hurtful policies, and they consider positive statements about minorities to be politically motivated. Also, they argue that MAGA plasters over centuries of wrongdoing and seeks to repair the breached walls of white supremacy.

An inclusive interpretation of MAGA

Before discussing criticisms of MAGA, I must first describe the inclusive interpretation of the slogan. Those who oppose the president and his version of history would do well to acquaint themselves with this interpretation, just as MAGA supporters need to understand why the slogan provokes adverse reactions.

Scholars looking for precision will find the president's campaign manifesto to be a frustrating read. The lack of details, he touts, is what made him a great negotiator. Those who approach his book looking for precision concerning when America was great will also be disappointed.

According to candidate Trump's manifesto, a great America responds to the voice of the people, creates jobs, accepts good trade deals, has a strong and feared military, protects against illegal immigration, ends birthright citizenship (this discussion includes his only mention of slavery and American Indians), protects the right to bear arms, protects traditional values, reforms tax codes, education and healthcare, resists lobbyists and special interest groups and secures affordable energy resources.[25] Trump repeatedly refers to the whole of American history as something of which to be proud. However, there are few specifically praised events or persons before Ronald Reagan – suggesting that his presidency coincided with the apogee of American greatness.

Another bone of contention relates to inclusivity: For whom was historical America great? To those who say Trump would be bad for women and minorities, he claimed many supported him because his business record showed a consistent policy of inclusivity, fairness and advancement.[26] His manifesto even employed inclusive language like 'all Americans'.[27]

In his so-called 'New Deal for African Americans' speech (26 October 2016), candidate Trump said 'Together, we will have a government of, by and for the people. And we will Make America Great Again For All Americans'.[28] In his Inaugural Address (20 January 2017), he praised the 'great national effort to rebuild our country and to restore its promise for all of our people'.[29] Finally, in a State of the Union Address (30 January 2018), he said, 'we have gone forward with a clear vision and a righteous mission – to make America great again for all Americans'.[30]

Inclusivity featured strongly in several speeches at the 2016 Republican National Convention (RNC). Darrell Scott, an African American pastor of New Spirit Revival Center in Cleveland Heights, Ohio, passionately argued for Trump. Scott is also the CEO of the National Diversity Coalition for Trump. Democratic policies harm minorities, he argues. He proudly appealed to history and the founders as he called for restored greatness. Scott's version of MAGA claimed to be both internationally and domestically inclusive: 'the greater that America is, the greater the entire world becomes'. Trump wants to get the 'best deal for all Americans', and he can 'become a president that everyone can be proud of'.[31]

Similarly, Mark Burns's speech to the RNC highlighted unity. As an African American minister at The Harvest Praise & Worship Center of Easley in South Carolina, Burns has become a vocal and steadfast supporter of Trump. *Yahoo! News* included him in a list of '16 people who shaped the 2016 election', and *Time* called him 'Trump's Top Pastor'.[32] Burns called out 'race-baiting Democrats' who sow division to keep power. Their policies, he claims, hurt the African American community. He 'declared to the whole world and to the Republican party, that under Donald Trump . . . all lives matter. . . . And that means black lives, white lives, Hispanic lives, Asian lives, Christian lives, Muslim lives'. He then led the audience in saying, 'all lives matter'. The crowd then interrupted, enthusiastically chanting, 'all lives matter'. His speech highlighted Trump's concern for the oppressed:

> Donald Trump is not going to pander after no one race, his heart is after the human race, and together, together, shout 'together' . . . not as black Americans, white Americans, brown Americans, yellow Americans or red Americans, but just as Americans. And together as Americans, we will get to the Promised Land.[33]

Red, white and blue matter more than the colour of one's skin in Burns's America. Both Scott and Burns have continued their support for Trump.

Other important figures like Newt Gingrich, David Horowitz and Corey Lewandowski, have all argued that MAGA was vague because it is inclusive. If this is the real Trump, they argue, then the media peddles fake news. According to this reasoning, there is an implied 'for all Americans' at the end of every 'Make America Great Again'.[34]

An exclusive interpretation of MAGA

In contrast to the previous interpretation, many believe MAGA is exclusive. Consider the speech announcing Trump's candidacy. Sub-par immigrants already in the nation were the main domestic threat – also insinuating that Islamic terrorists might be sneaking across the Southern border.[35] Once in office, Trump's exclusionary policies and rhetoric, like the ban on persons from predominantly Muslim countries or comments about 'shithole countries', revealed that MAGA benefits Christians or those from wealthy white countries. Additionally, critics are alarmed by the affinity between Trump and authoritarian strongmen who have a tenuous relationship with human rights, democracy, free press and the rule of law.

Some suspect Trump is moving the country from the centuries-old bipartisan civil-religious model of nationalism to a narrower form of religious nationalism that favours conservative Christians. The Right justifies this prioritisation of Christianity in public life, in part, by appeals to an increasingly totalitarian form of secular nationalism.[36] The choice of Mike Pence for vice president sent a clear message that the administration would champion the interests of evangelical and conservative culture warriors.[37]

Trump's Twitter feed is a go-to source, showing who he thinks threatens American greatness – and thus who might be adversely affected by MAGA or excluded from it. *The New York Times* recorded '598 People, Places and Things Trump Has Insulted on Twitter' (last updated 24 May 2019).[38] Trump's tweets routinely disparage women and people of colour.[39] When open racists endorse him, the president is slow to distance himself, if he distances himself at all.

Another argument for an exclusivist MAGA is Trump's exclusivist supporters. Consider Roy Moore, the controversial former chief justice of the Alabama Supreme Court. In his bid for the US Senate, he said, 'I want to be part of the leadership team that will make America great again'.[40] Even before allegations of sexual misconduct with teenagers, Moore was controversial for (among other things) his defence of the public display of the Ten Commandments and for his views on race and LGBTQ+ rights. Moore's version of MAGA, it would appear, is Judeo-Christian in its foundation, gives preferential treatment to whites and does not respect sexual minorities.

Trump's nationalistic appeals are also worrisome. 'Americans are highly nationalistic', write J. Christopher Soper and Joel S. Fetzer, and religious Americans score only a little higher on the nationalism scale than non-religious Americans. From the founding, Americans (to varying degrees and in differing ways) have attached religious significance to the nation.[41] However, nationalism raises issues of race. This racial dimension is particularly salient for Native Americans and African Americans who were long deprived of political rights. Minorities, especially, worry that MAGA involves a nostalgic return to a time when whites did not have to take the rights of minorities seriously.

Philip Gorski recently argued that a secularised form of white Christian nationalism played an important part in the election of Donald Trump. He summarises the works of other scholars in the field:

> Roughly speaking, 'white Christian nationalism' (WCN) is the view that America was built by and for white Christians, and that if you are not a white Christian, you are also not fully or truly American. In the bluntest terms, real Americans are white Christians and vice versa.

What does MAGA mean?

It is not that white evangelicals are fully aware of this assumption: 'it is probably more akin to what fellow sociologist Arlie Hochschild calls a "deep story", a half-conscious narrative that tacitly structures our perceptions about past, present, and future'. Trump then buttresses nostalgic narratives with 'victimization, messianism, and anti-elitism'.[42] This deep story starts with the Pilgrims in 1620 and ends with the secular assault on religion and American values.

More worrying still, a growing and vocal minority on the Right openly promotes white nationalism and white rights. Richard Spencer, an Alt-Right leader, describes himself as an atheist who thinks society still needs religion to flourish.[43] Shortly after Trump's election, Spencer led a crowd in 'Hail Trump, hail our people, hail victory!' Some audience members raised a Nazi salute. He described a 'conquer or die' fight for white existence. Many in the Alt-Right promote the old idea that multiculturalism will bring about 'white genocide' and that 'anti-racist' means 'anti-white'.[44] The Alt-Right is animated by vocal and sometimes violent opposition by Antifa – loosely organised counter-protesters opposed to resurgent fascism.

Spencer's arguments about white identity invoke history at every step: 'America was until this past generation a white country, designed for ourselves and our posterity. It is our creation, it is our inheritance, and it belongs to us'.[45] He supports 'peaceful ethnic redistribution', encouraging all immigrants to return to their 'true homes' (except for Europeans who rightfully possess America).[46] When asked on National Public Radio if 'Make America White Again' was an appropriate slogan, Spencer said, 'I don't have a huge problem with that'.[47] President Trump, although not a part of the Alt-Right, is considered by many of them to be a fellow traveller.[48]

The MAGA time machine

Perhaps it is useful to think of MAGA as a time machine. It claims to move the country forward by going backwards. According to James Poniewozik in *Audience of One: Donald Trump, Television, and the Fracturing of America*, Trump's slogan 'was a nostalgia act. . . . It was strategically vague. Maybe America was last great in the 1980s, or in the 1950s, or before'.[49] In the end, he argues, we do not need precision because Trump is not precise. 'So you don't have to come out and say who "Make America Great Again" is for. You just have to set the dial on the time machine and see who climbs in'.[50] Although the MAGA travel brochure is hazy on details, many on the Left think the destination seems troubling.

The metaphor works another way. Critics observing the MAGA time machine make assumptions about where the individual passengers are headed. One poor white passenger might think he is headed back to economic prosperity. The Left accuses him of buying a ticket to male supremacy. Another female passenger might be wanting to return to a time when Christians were not losing in the courts. She is accused of purchasing a ticket to a country that keeps out immigrants. These passengers would not deny that an alarming number of racists have climbed aboard the MAGA time machine. They may wonder why overt racists have not been kicked off the ride. There might even be a civil war in the time machine – Religious Right, Alt-Right and Libertarian passengers vying for the controls. But many are tired of being defined by the worst elements of the MAGA crowd. This frustration confirms the sense that Trump understands and defends them.

Charitable critics on the Left and Right have cautioned against reducing all Trump supporters to the worst stereotype. Trump supporters are frequently dehumanised in the national press, and the media wonders why they seek refuge in the president.[51] 'Othering' Trump supporters keeps them mysterious and incomprehensible (or I should say, not worth comprehending).[52] Further, 'othering' Trump supporters (slightly under half of the country) is put forward as Exhibit A in the case that the Left has become as vile as the president they oppose.

To move forward, Van Jones said, 'Liberals must accept that every Trump voter is not a white supremacist. But conservatives should be worried that so many white supremacists are Trump voters'.[53] Similarly, Arthur C. Brooks said, 'Anyone who can't tell the difference between an ordinary Bernie Sanders supporter and a Stalinist revolutionary, or between Donald Trump's average voter and a Nazi, is either willfully ignorant or needs to get out of the house more'.[54] Jones and Brooks would likely agree that Trump benefits when his supporters are indiscriminately demonised.

Notes

1 Thomas Tillam's poem, 'Uppon the First Sight of New-England', written 29 June 1638 (John Davis Papers, 1627–1846 [Ms. N-1097.4c] MHS.
2 See Andrew R. Murphy, *Prodigal Nation: Moral Decline and Divine Punishment from New England to 9/11* (Oxford: Oxford University Press, 2011).
3 Chris Hedges, *America: The Farewell Tour* (New York: Simon & Schuster, 2018); Michael L. Brown, *Saving a Sick America: A Prescription for Moral and Cultural Transformation* (Nashville: Thomas Nelson, 2017).
4 Robert P. Jones, *The End of White Christian America* (New York: Simon & Schuster, 2016), 86. Statistics from the 2015 Public Religion Research Institute's Americans Values Survey.
5 Kayleigh McEnany, *The New American Revolution: The Making of a Populist Movement* (New York: Threshold, 2018). In 2020, McEnany became the White House Press Secretary.
6 Jonathan Wilson-Hartgrove, *Revolution of Values: Reclaiming Public Faith for the Common Good* (Downers Grove: InterVarsity, 2019).

What does MAGA mean?

7 On this, see Diane Enns, *The Violence of Victimhood* (University Park: Penn State University Press, 2012).
8 Donald J. Trump, *Crippled America: How to Make America Great Again* (New York: Threshold, 2015).
9 Philip S. Gorski, *American Babylon: Christianity and Democracy Before and After Trump* (New York: Routledge, 2020), 112.
10 Mark Charles and Soong-Chan Rah, *Unsettling Truths: The Ongoing, Dehumanizing Legacy of the Doctrine of Discovery* (Downers Grove: InterVarsity, 2019), 78–80.
11 Margot Sanger-Katz, 'When Was America Greatest?', *The New York Times* (26 Apr 2016). Online: www.nytimes.com/2016/04/26/upshot/when-was-america-greatest.html. Retrieved 6 Mar 2020.
12 James Poniewozik, *Audience of One: Donald Trump, Television, and the Fracturing of America* (New York: Liveright, 2019), 214.
13 Michael D'Antonio, *Never Enough: Donald Trump and the Pursuit of Success* (New York: St. Martin's Press, 2015), 13.
14 Ibid., 341.
15 Donald J. Trump and Tony Schwartz, *Trump: The Art of the Deal* (1987 Repr.; New York: Ballantine Books, 2015), 58.
16 Donald J. Trump and Dave Shiflett, *The America We Deserve* (Los Angeles: Renaissance, 2000), Kindle Loc. 628–9.
17 Roderick P. Hart, *Trump and Us: What He Says and Why People Listen* (Cambridge: Cambridge University Press, 2020), 58.
18 Donald J. Trump, 'Remarks by President Trump at a Reception for National African American History Month' (21 Feb 2019). Online: www.whitehouse.gov/briefings-statements/remarks-president-trump-reception-national-african-american-history-month/. Retrieved 20 Mar 2020.
19 Hart, *Trump and Us*, 17.
20 Ralph Reed, *For God and Country: The Christian Case for Trump* (Washington, DC: Regnery, 2020), 36.
21 Ruth Graham, 'Church of the Donald: Never Mind Fox. Trump's Most Reliable Media Mouthpiece Is Now Christian TV', *Politico* (May/June 2018). Online: www.politico.com/magazine/story/2018/04/22/trump-christian-evangelical-conservatives-television-tbn-cbn-218008. Retrieved 11 Feb 2020; Elizabeth Dias and Diane Tsai, 'Meet Donald Trump's Top Pastor', *Time*. Online: https://time.com/trump-pastor. Retrieved 11 Feb 2020. Many minority ministers have characterised Trump supporters as intoxicated by their proximity to power; 'Open Letter To Trump's Preachers' (3 Aug 2018), *Black Theology Project*. Online: https://btpbase.org/open-letter-to-trumps-preachers/. Retrieved 23 June 2020; cf. 'Message to Black Clergy: Think of Trump's Rhetoric Before Meeting with Him', *Ebony* (27 Nov 2015). Online: www.ebony.com/news/message-to-black-clergy-think-of-trumps-rhetoric-before-meeting-with-him-333/. Retrieved 23 Nov 2020.
22 Sarah Posner, *Unholy: Why Evangelicals Worship at the Altar of Donald Trump* (New York: Random House, 2020), 63.
23 Paula White-Cain's comments on a 1 November 2018 special 'Faith for Our Nation' edition of *Believer's Voice of Victory*. 'Today: Addressing the Spirit of Racism'. Online: www.kcm.org/watch/tv-broadcast/addressing-the-spirit-racism. Retrieved 1 July 2020.
24 Stephen E. Strang, *Trump Aftershock: The President's Seismic Impact on Culture and Faith in America* (Lake Mary, FL: Charisma House, 2018), xv.

24 *What does MAGA mean?*

25 See in particular, Trump, *Crippled America*, 163–5.
26 Trump, *Crippled America*, 4–5. On the relationship that led to Paula White-Cain becoming his spiritual advisor, see Paula White-Cain, *Something Greater: Finding Triumph Over Trials* (New York: Hachette, 2019).
27 Trump, *Crippled America*, 5, 100–1.
28 Transcript can be found online: Tim Hains, 'Trump Proposes "New Deal for Black America" in Charlotte', *Real Clear Politics* (26 Oct 2016). Online: www.realclearpolitics.com/video/2016/10/26/trump_proposes_new_deal_for_black_america_in_charlotte.html. Retrieved 28 Jan 2020.
29 Donald J. Trump, 'The Inaugural Address' (20 Jan 2017). Online: www.whitehouse.gov/briefings-statements/the-inaugural-address/. Retrieved 2 Feb 2020.
30 Donald J. Trump, 'State of the Union Address' (30 Jan 2018). Online: www.whitehouse.gov/briefings-statements/president-donald-j-trumps-state-union-address/. Retrieved 2 Feb 2020.
31 Darrell Scott, 'Speech to the Republican National Convention' (20 July 2016), Cleveland, Ohio.
32 Jerry Adler, '16 People Who Shaped the 2016 Election: Pastor Mark Burns', *Yahoo! News* (24 Oct 2016). Online: www.yahoo.com/news/16-people-who-shaped-the-2016-election-pastor-mark-burns-171839357.html. Retrieved 23 June 2020. Elizabeth Dias and Diane Tsai, 'Meet Donald Trump's Top Pastor', *Time*. Online: https://time.com/trump-pastor/. Retrieved 23 June 2020.
33 Mark Burns, Speech to the Republican National Convention (20 July 2016), Cleveland, Ohio.
34 Newt Gingrich, *Understanding Trump* (New York: Hatchet, 2017), 39; David Horowitz, *Big Agenda: President Trump's Plan to Save America* (West Palm Beach, FL: Humanix, 2017), 154–5; *Campaign for President: The Managers Look at 2016* (Lanham, MD: Rowman & Littlefield, 2017), 163.
35 Time Staff, 'Here's Donald Trump's Presidential Announcement Speech', *Time* (16 June 2015). Online: https://time.com/3923128/donald-trump-announcement-speech/. Retrieved 1 July 2020.
36 On civil-religious nationalism, religious nationalism and secular nationalism, see J. Christopher Soper and Joel S. Fetzer, *Religion and Nationalism in Global Perspective* (Cambridge: Cambridge University Press, 2018), 1–72.
37 For differing viewpoints on Pence, see Tom LoBianco, *Piety & Power: Mike Pence and the Taking of the White House* (New York: Dey St., 2019); Leslie Montgomery, *The Faith of Mike Pence* (Kensington, PA: Whitaker, 2019).
38 Jasmine C. Lee and Kevin Quealy, 'The 598 People, Places and Things Donald Trump Has Insulted on Twitter: A Complete List', *The New York Times*. Online: www.nytimes.com/interactive/2016/01/28/upshot/donald-trump-twitter-insults.html. Retrieved 1 July 2020.
39 See citations of Twitter in Sider, *The Spiritual Danger of Donald Trump*.
40 Roy Moore, 'God Gave America a Second Chance Last November', *AL.com* (13 Aug 2017). Online: www.al.com/opinion/2017/08/roy_moore_god_gave_america_a_s.html. Retrieved 1 July 2020.
41 Soper and Fetzer, *Religion and Nationalism in Global Perspective*, 57.
42 Gorski, *American Babylon*, 108, 109, 112; Andrew L. Whitehead and Samuel L. Perry, *Taking America Back for God: Christian Nationalism in the United States* (Oxford: Oxford University Press, 2020).
43 David McAfee discussion with Richard Spencer, 'The Alt Right and Secular Humanism' (2017). Online: https://altright.com/2017/01/23/the-alt-right-and-secular-humanism/. Retrieved 1 July 2020.

44 Posner, *Unholy*, 129–30.
45 Daniel Lombrosoyni and Yoni Applebaul '"Hail Trump!": White Nationalists Salute the President-Elect', *The Atlantic* (21 Nov 2016). Online: www.theatlantic.com/politics/archive/2016/11/richard-spencer-speech-npi/508379/. Retrieved 1 July 2020.
46 Spencer, 'The Alt Right and Secular Humanism'.
47 *The Atlantic*, 'Rebranding White Nationalism: Inside the Alt-Right'. Online: https://vimeo.com/196594487. Retrieved 1 July 2020.
48 Spencer, 'The Alt Right and Secular Humanism'.
49 Poniewozik, *Audience of One*, 212.
50 Ibid., 215.
51 For examples, see Hart, *Trump and Us*, 117–40.
52 Hart, *Trump and Us*, 151.
53 Jones, *Beyond the Messy Truth*, 102.
54 Brooks, *Love Your Enemies*, 14.

3 Make America great again

The burden of memory

Cultural warriors – on both the Left and Right – carry around a burden of grievances that they hope to offload someday. For those who supported President Trump, these grievances might be political, personal, economic, cultural or religious. Variety reigns. Tim Alberta memorably called the president 'a canopy of discontent under which the grudging masses could congregate to air their grievances about a nation they no longer recognized and a government they no longer trusted'.[1]

Those so burdened are joined by historical pilgrims. Protestant supporters of MAGA might envision continuity with Ronald Reagan or Billy Graham. Figures like George Washington, Abraham Lincoln and Martin Luther King Jr. might also appear. Some will argue they strive to walk in the footsteps of the Pilgrims and Puritans who went to extraordinary lengths to please God in the midst of a wicked and corrupt generation. Historical companionship lightens the burden.

Many of these grievances relate to how history is handled. The Right claims the Left is unwilling to acknowledge what went right in American history. As the diplomat Danny Toma argued, 'To suggest that maybe, just maybe, our forefathers got more right than wrong was "deplorable"'.[2] The iconoclastic Left, many argue, does not value historical understanding nor the nuance that places persons within their historical context. Historical figures fall short of the progressive platform, and thus their images must be defaced with all the zeal of a chisel-wielding reformer.

The Protestant Right's baggage contains several laws and landmark court rulings.[3] In 1954, the Johnson Amendment prohibited non-profit 501(c)(3) organisations from publicly opposing or supporting candidates. In 1962, in *Engel v. Vitale*, the Supreme Court declared prayer in public school to be unconstitutional. The following year they decided against mandatory Bible reading in public schools in *Abington v. Schempp*. A decade later, *Roe v.*

Wade (1973) allowed for abortion rights. Additionally, from 1993 to 2014, the number of white Protestants declined from 51% to 32%.[4]

Then a series of rulings decriminalised same-sex acts (*Lawrence v. Texas* [2003]) and extended, incrementally, marriage rights to same-sex couples (*Romer v. Evans* [1996] and *Obergefell v. Hodges* [2015]).[5] A host of recent cases touched on the extent of religious liberty, particularly when a more libertine sexual ethic (growing out of the sexual revolution of the 1960s) collided with deeply held religious beliefs (e.g. *Priests for Life v. HHS* [2012]; *Burwell v. Hobby Lobby* [2014]; *Masterpiece Cakeshop, Ltd. v. Colorado Civil Rights Commission* [2018]).

In *Sacred Liberty*, Steven Waldman said the Supreme Court seems 'inconsistent and confused' on religious liberty.

> [O]n balance, the Court over the past fifty years has dramatically expanded and strengthened religious freedom, but not in the ways one might expect. The general philosophy that has emerged is that government involvement in overt religion should be limited [often angering the Right], but also that, as a society, we should bend over backward to make sure that secular laws don't inadvertently do any damage to religious freedom [often angering the Left].[6]

This situation gives both sides in the culture war cause to celebrate and reasons to groan. Both are victors; both feel victimised.

Even when conservative Christians emerged victoriously, the fact that the courts were necessary heightened their defensiveness and affirmed desires to restore America. Enter Trump's election manifesto: 'It seems like every week there is a negative ruling on some issue having to do with Christianity. I think it's outrageous, totally outrageous'.[7] Conservative Christians wanted a strongman who would upset the power structures, and Trump effortlessly stepped into that role.[8] At the January 2020 'Evangelicals for Trump' rally, the president said 'the day I took office . . . the Federal Government's war on religion came to an abrupt end'. His protection was rewarded. A 2020 Pew Research Center survey showed that white evangelicals overwhelmingly prized a president who 'stands up for people w/ your religious beliefs' – and this protection was more important than personal morality or religious beliefs.

This Pew survey also found that although a majority of white evangelical Protestants (57%) and black Protestants (51%) believe Trump's election was 'part of God's plan', very few (13% and 5% respectively) say he was chosen because God endorsed his policies. A similar pattern is evident in views about President Obama's election,[9] suggesting that Protestants view elections through the lens of general providence, not primarily special providence. God is involved in elections because God is involved in everything (general), not because Obama or Trump had uniquely curried favour with God (special).

The desire for restored greatness predates Trump. In *The Church of Us vs. Them*, David E. Fitch argues that for many Trump supporters, 'Make America Great Again' builds on decades of work to Make America Christian Again.[10] Notice how 'Again' features in the title of D. James Kennedy's influential *What If America Were a Christian Nation Again?*[11] Kennedy's providential narrative stretched from antiquity to the present, downplaying American Christian complicity in racism, sexism and exploitation. Also, judging by the number of recent patriotic Bibles, little separates 'Make America Biblical' from 'Make the Bible American'.

Those lamenting a lost Christian nation indulge in narratives of decline. Pollster George Barna and activist David Barton speak of a looming 'Dark Ages' because Americans have turned their back on the beliefs that animated the Pilgrims. 'America has been one of the greatest nations in human history', and repentance and renewal 'is necessary if we want to attain such greatness again'.[12]

America's 'founding' as a 'Christian nation' is particularly controversial – not least because most engaging in the debate aim to enlist the past in present battles. They thrust questions onto the past and draw clear inferences for modern policy. Partisans often seek (and therefore see) clear answers.[13] Partisan organisations like David Barton's WallBuilders or the Freedom From Religion Foundation often speak as if they alone carry the founders' torch. However, I find it hard to imagine that the founders intended either of their incompatible Americas.

Historian John Fea finds the idea of a Christian nation to be theologically and historically problematic. However, he argues that 'until the 1970s, Americans – evangelicals and non-evangelicals alike – believed that they were living in a Christian nation'.[14] If Fea is correct, then the attempt to restore America to its Christian founding is deeply misguided. However, he also acknowledges the loss of a consensus since the 1970s. In other words, those pining for restoration are not imagining a long history where Americans assumed a Christian nation with Christian values.[15]

Many critics argue that the Religious Right is fundamentally changing America. Whatever the merits of their analysis, the argument will fail to convince Christian conservatives for one simple reason – the argument feels like gaslighting. 'Gaslighting' is a form of mental manipulation whereby the sufferer is made to doubt their suffering. The term is often used to describe how those who experience racism are then told they are not experiencing racism. In this form of gaslighting, progressives denigrate conservatives for fundamentally altering society while simultaneously applauding how rapidly society changed. Progressives call conservative Christians unreasonable for making slippery slope arguments and then celebrate how sharply the slope trends upwards (from their perspective). To the Right, this feels like doublespeak. Those on the Right are told they do not really see the changes that have swept the country in their own lifetime. Decades ago, many warned that Christians would be dragged into court for adhering to traditional values. Those reviled as paranoid are now revered as prophetic. 'Progress' becomes confirmation that the Right should have dug in its heels decades ago. Now they fight with the vehemence of those regaining valuable ground.

On top of this frustration over the rapidly changing religious landscape, the agents of change deny that they persecute those who do not keep pace. However, the long and sordid history of fighting over religion teaches an important lesson: those who persecute rarely think of what they are doing as 'persecution'. Persecution denial is as old as persecution.[16] Persecutors almost always dress their actions in the garb of righteousness. Catholics did this to Lutherans, Lutherans to Calvinists, Calvinists to the irreligious. Now, it is argued, the irreligious persecute the religious and then hide the body behind banners that point to an egalitarian tomorrow. When the persecutor denies persecuting, this exacerbates the sense of injustice. We must set aside questions about any specific act of persecution claimed by the Religious Right. However, it is undeniable that many think they are persecuted. Christians, they argue, are the only group who are mocked for feeling persecuted. For other protected groups, every assertion of injustice should be believed and acted upon.

Similarly, many economically deprived whites despise elite depictions of them. They feel a similar gaslighting when people speak of white privilege. They may not deny that this privilege exists for some, but they do not feel as if they (or their community) have benefited from their skin colour. After they experience unemployment, addiction, dismal education prospects, shortened life expectancy and neglected communities, the Left wraps insult around accusations of privilege. When those on the Left accuse, *en masse*, those on the Right of 'white supremacy', this prompts the same reaction as when those on the Right call those on the Left 'baby killers' – immediate denial followed by either the cessation of dialogue or the escalation of conflict. Several African American leaders have recently argued that poor whites are worthy of far more sympathy and far less demonisation.[17]

Many Americans feel as if the policies of the Left have personally harmed them. Wealthy, educated elites benefit from globalisation and the rapidly changing social and ethical mores. However, many conservatives feel that progressive policies have led to the loss of jobs, the breakdown of communities and a general sense of homelessness. Those adversely impacted are told that global citizenship is beneficial and that progress should be embraced, but they feel bludgeoned by increased immigration and by open and permissive societies. Further, they cannot express their sense of loss because the Left will call them racist xenophobes. From this perspective, the Left is both perpetrator and judge. The Left harmed much of America and then pronounced a damning verdict over the victim.[18]

When poor white and religiously conservative identities intersect, these compound feelings of marginalisation. When their sense of persecution is invalidated or mocked, this further embitters them against a large portion of the country. They may even wear insults as badges of honour – 'bitter clingers' and 'basket of deplorables', for example. For many, MAGA acknowledges how far the cultural landscape has shifted. It acknowledges how economic prospects look bleak. It validates their sense of persecution. More importantly, MAGA promises to do something about it.

Emotion is key to Trump supporters. Roderick P. Hart, a professor of government at the University of Texas who works on political communication, explores 'four primary emotions that drove many voters into the Trump camp'.

> Donald Trump knew that many Americans felt *ignored* so he acknowledged them with an accessible, populist style. He knew that some folks felt *trapped* and he uplifted them via emotion-filled storytelling. Others of his constituents felt *besieged* – by elites, especially by the media – so he offered them public therapy by becoming an alternative news source for them. Mr. Trump also sensed that many Americans were *weary* of the political establishment so he used his distinct personality and a barrage of tweets to energize them.[19]

Ignored, trapped, besieged, weary; the vitriol directed at all things Trump rubs salt in these emotional wounds. The Left ignores the wounds and hates the cure. If the salt pains MAGA supporters, it also preserves their resolve. In other words, hatred makes re-election possible, namely the hatred directed at those who sought refuge in Trump.[20]

Hart notes the appeal of Trump's reclamation narrative. His stories – often reminiscent of a repetitive and hyperbolic chat with an old friend over a pint – appealed to the deep hurts of many, and 'Trump presented himself as a curative'.[21] If you dig beneath the offensive language,

> I suggest that you will also find narratives designed to heal the wounds – both real and imagined – of Trump's supporters. Although it is easy to dismiss all narratives as mere fiction, Donald Trump knew better and he became president because of what he knew.[22]

The Left denied the ways in which their attitudes and policies hurt many, but Trump saw these wounds and pursued the aggressor.

In the rest of this chapter, I attempt to understand the contours of historical memory for those who want to restore American greatness. Most authors acknowledge racism, sexism and exploitation in America's deep past. However, the admission of historical injustice is often cursory. The Right needs to understand why de-emphasising historical failures feels like a token admission of guilt that absolves whites from working towards justice in the present.

Make America Great Again Protestants are overwhelmingly white, theologically conservative and support the Republican platform. They do not see themselves as writing from a white perspective. Even though they might have a category for Black Theology, they would bristle at the charge that theirs is White Theology (they simply practice 'theology'). However, critics might argue that their arguments reveal the dubious assumption that the white experience of Christianity and America is normative and therefore correct.

Those who desire to restore American greatness have a long list of what's wrong with America. The register of resentment differs depending on who is doing the grieving – and some do not see Trump as the solution. The following sketches illustrate the different roads one can travel on the quest to Make America Great Again.

Robert Jeffress

For many on the Religious Right, decline started with the Johnson Amendment, and candidate Trump promised to do away with it. On 4 May 2017, he signed 'an executive order to follow through on that pledge'. It would 'prevent the Johnson Amendment from interfering with your First Amendment rights'.[23] The following month, Dr Robert Jeffress – pastor of First Baptist Church in Dallas and one of Trump's earliest ministerial supporters – took full advantage of liberation.

Jeffress is one of the foremost evangelical defenders of Donald Trump, part of what historian John Fea has dubbed the 'court evangelicals' – the others being Jerry Falwell Jr., James Dobson, Johnnie Moore, Ralph Reed, Paula White, Gary Bauer and Mark Burns.[24] Former presidential candidate Mike Huckabee called Jeffress the pastor 'of one of the most influential churches of Christendom'. Jeffress has a long history of political commentary, writing books like *Twilight's Last Gleaming: How America's Last Days Can be Your Best Days*.[25] The book sounds like the product of a merger between Tim LaHaye and Joel Osteen. Perhaps *Left Behind* and *Your Best Life Now* are a good place to start with the Protestant Right and Trump – for prophetic apocalypticism and prosperity preaching are frequently used to support the president.

When President Trump lifted the chains of government restriction, Jeffress's church celebrated Freedom Sunday (25 June 2017). Patriotic rallies are common in some streams of American evangelicalism. The overt support for the president made this service unique. The church choir debuted 'Make America Great Again' – a song written by Gary Moore. It emphasises freedom, unity, destiny and national pride but never alludes to God. The song contained almost no details about what this great America will look like or when America saw its finest hour.

Trump's faithful ministers have been amply rewarded. Jeffress, for example, prayed at the opening of the United States Embassy in Jerusalem. His words linked biblical with modern history, thanking God for a president who stands with God, is on the 'right side of history' and will receive a blessing for blessing Israel.

A recent book, *Praying for America: 40 Inspiring Stories and Prayers for Our Nation*, prepares conservative Christians for the 2020 election. American greatness depends on pastoral boldness. Each chapter follows a pattern. He presents a historical vignette followed by contemporary application and then closes with a prayer. The book spans American history from the Pilgrims to the present, occasionally calling out the nation for its racial failures. Jeffress presents a relatively seamless picture of the past, present and future. God and Satan have been at work throughout. The protagonists change (the Pilgrims, George Washington, John Adams, Sam Houston, Abraham Lincoln, Mike Huckabee and so on), and the antagonists change (the British, godless French revolutionaries, Confederates, Santa Anna, atheists, communists, activist judges, Islamic terrorists, Antifa and so on).

In prayer 22, 'To Know History and Learn from It', Jeffress reflects on remembering God's works:

> Creating memorials [as the biblical Joshua did] to remember how God has helped us in the past bolsters our faith and brings glory to God. We also establish monuments to remember either the heroism or the foolishness of our forebears. We honor significant people of the past, but we neither idolize nor demonize them. And we certainly don't forget them. Rather, we take a long, honest look. This motivates us to right action for the future.

Remembering the past is essential for 'any civilization to survive'; forgetting leaves individuals as 'easy prey for Satan's schemes'.[26] The implications for the debate over national monuments are clear. Statues, even of flawed humans, are silent teachers. The health of the nation depends on listening to them.

Cal Thomas

Cal Thomas, an evangelical and famous news correspondent, has written on national decline in *America's Expiration Date* (2020): 'the nation that I love is in danger of losing its greatness'.[27] He explores 'the causes of the decline and fall of great empires and nation-states of the past and examine[s] what we can learn that might ward off a similar fate for the United States'.[28] Thomas wants to forestall a funeral in 2026 – the 250th anniversary of the nation's founding. Empires tend to collapse around that age.

Americans continuously ask God to bless America. But 'Why should he?' Israel is the 'only nation ever to enjoy a covenant relationship with God'.[29] Rather than moving into increasing blessedness, decadence is here, and decline awaits. Pedlars of blessedness often ignore America's manifold sins: 'Ancient Israel was destroyed for sins similar to ours'.[30] Decline quickened pace in the 1950s. His book counters the 'revisionist variety [of history] taught in many public schools and universities'.[31] Little mention is made of the sins of racism, sexism and economic exploitation that form part of American history.

Thomas evidences a certain ambivalence about America's past. He overviews history from Columbus to the Pilgrims to George Washington.

> Those who established the new nation believed they had a higher purpose than making money. . . . Many believed, *rightly or wrongly*, that they had a divine purpose, and they said so on many occasions. *Whether they actually were fulfilling God's will, they thought they were*, and that in itself motivated them to stick with it as they confronted and eventually conquered the many challenges ahead [italics added].[32]

Belief in a divine purpose may have been misguided (not to mention lethal), but this belief fostered a drive towards greatness. Renewal requires reconciliation with the God of American history.

Os Guinness

Os Guinness is a popular English apologist who earned his doctorate at Oxford. He has a large following in the United States through public speaking, fellowships and publications. Many of his books diagnose the moral and theological health of the United States. *Last Call for Liberty* (2018) says, 'America's genius for freedom has become its Achilles heel and a leading source of America's divisions and potential destruction'.[33] Trump is 'the consequence of a crisis and not the cause', and the desire to restore greatness does not lead to the sanctification of the president.[34]

How did a nation with such a promising start get here? America broke the covenant made with God in the 1620s and 1630s.

> The current parties to the American covenant have multiplied by many millions, but the same conditions, the same open-endedness of the project, and the same challenge of the experiment confront Americans as

they did the Jews and the Puritans. . . . In sum, two truths confront Americans in every generation: The great experiment is conditional, and the citizens of the American republic are responsible.[35]

Guinness says, 'A founding creates a nation's DNA'. As a result, 'No one can hope to make America great again in any direction without understanding what made America great in the first place'.[36] The covenant, the Constitution and limited power propelled America to greatness.

Repentance and recovenanting are the way forward.

> *By recovenanting and going back first, the United States is in fact able to go forward.* Properly understood, recovenanting is progressive. Covenantalism and constitutionalism acknowledge the past with gratitude, but they do not remain in the past. There is no golden age they wish to return to.[37]

By repenting for covenant unfaithfulness, Americans can finally deal with their past.

After repentance, 'America's abiding curse of racism can finally be resolved and not perpetuated forever'.[38] He laments at several points

> the gap between the American genius for freedom and the reality of slavery, and thus between America's ideals and self-image as the 'land of the free' and the sordid realities of the long degradation of the African slaves and then of African Americans. . . . The same was true of other inconsistencies and distortions from the founder's America – supremely the treatment of women, of Native Americans, and the treatment of other nations through America's sense of manifest destiny and exceptionalism.[39]

American history grounds shame and hope – but he focuses on the better moments. Racism, sexism and greed disfigure history and distort Christianity. However, past generations knew obedience to God's word was the secret to greatness.

Eric Metaxas

Eric Metaxas is a Yale-educated author, radio host and speaker who frequently writes on history and Christianity. He was raised in the Greek Orthodox faith, for which he still holds deep respect, but has long attended Calvary-St. George's Episcopal Church in Manhattan. His writings focus on what unites Christian traditions. His biographies of William Wilberforce

(2007), Dietrich Bonhoeffer (2011) and Martin Luther (2017) have all been widely praised and criticised (especially Bonhoeffer). He has also published three collections of short biographies of heroic men and women (2013, 2015, 2020) 'And the Secret of Their Greatness' (as the subtitles read). Metaxas has also been an ardent supporter of President Trump.

If You Can Keep It: The Forgotten Promise of American Liberty (2016) begins with Os Guinness's golden triangle of freedom: Freedom requires virtue; virtue requires faith; faith requires freedom. All three are imperilled.[40]

Metaxas is an unashamed advocate of American exceptionalism, but this exceptionalism, properly understood, blesses the entire world.[41] In their grateful pride, Americans must not succumb to 'jingoism or nationalism'.[42] He worries that Americans have lost the ability to celebrate 'the heroic in general'. Previous generations were spurred on to greatness by reading *Plutarch's Lives*,[43] even though the beliefs and behaviours of these pagans were not always worth emulating.

Beyond forgetting heroes, many Americans demonise them.[44]

> Denigrating heroes, or simply failing to venerate them, has a cynical and toxic effect on the young generation, and we have now had fifty years in which we have neglected this 'habit of the heart' so vital to our free way of life.[45]

Cynical iconoclasts corrupt society.

Of all the *Make America Great Again* authors described in this book, Metaxas has the longest section on confronting national evils. Although much criticism of America is destructive, 'seeing these bad things about ourselves was an extraordinarily positive development'. Polarised historiography, not self-critique, was the problem. Some Americans only see America as 'the great savior of the world', others as 'the great villain on the world stage'. America and the world are hurt by this polarisation. 'To truly love America, one must somehow see both sides simultaneously'. When confronted with postcards celebrating a lynching, Americans 'must acknowledge this as part of our history. But we must also acknowledge our most heroic moments without waving them off as rare anomalies or as mere hypocrisy'. Americans should repent for some aspects of the past and rejoice over other parts. Balance will stave off a 'deeply distorted view' of history that is destructive to faith, freedom and virtue.[46]

People resemble what they revere. If they gaze fondly at Washington's greatness, they will be moved towards greatness. If they constantly point out the flaws in the past, they will become harsh and uncharitable persons. Metaxas does not, however, entertain the mirror conclusion: by revering racists, Americans will become racist.

Metaxas then turns to Scripture for guidance on how to love the nation. Scripture's commands to love enemies does not mean we 'love the evil in our enemies. He is telling us to love what is beyond that, to love the goodness in them that [God] sees and that he put there'. In the same way, love of country does not mean loving national evils. Love looks beyond the evil to what is good.[47]

In *principle*, Metaxas seems close to the *Make America Better* position described in Chapter 5. In *practice*, there is a wide gap between the positions. Let us examine two Americans commemorated at length in *If You Can Keep It*: George Whitefield and Abraham Lincoln.

Metaxas devotes about one-sixth of the book to George Whitefield, whose preaching, by any standard, profoundly shaped American history and identity. He mentions how Whitefield's message was egalitarian and socially levelling for both whites and blacks.[48] However, Metaxas omits the well-known fact that Whitefield owned many slaves and successfully advocated for the extension of slavery.[49] On account of slavery, the University of Pennsylvania announced in July 2020 that it would remove Whitefield's statue.[50]

Likewise, Metaxas lionised Lincoln. He praises Lincoln for his integrity and opposition to the evil of slavery but does not mention his vocal white supremacy. He notes how with the stroke of a pen, Lincoln bettered the condition of African Americans but fails to mention how that same pen deprived many Native Americans of land and life (see discussions in Chapter 4).[51]

For all Metaxas's words about confronting the past, he fails to do so for these 'great' men. He passionately argues for a balanced approach to America's failings, but his own histories show how easily the lamentable aspects of the past disappear in a fog of nostalgia.

Metaxas returns to many of these themes in his 2020 book, *Seven More Men: And the Secret of Their Greatness* (written with Anne Morse). This book offers short biographies of Martin Luther, George Whitefield, William Booth, George Washington Carver, Sergeant Alvin York, Alexander Solzhenitsyn and Billy Graham. Metaxas argues that 'ignorance of these lives . . . has contributed greatly to many of the problems facing us today'. These men had 'real flaws', but imperfection did not negate 'the value of all the good'. Further, 'lives are at stake in our failure to take a broad view' of flawed historical persons (p.10–11).

Although the chapter on Whitefield is dismissive of racism and slavery, Metaxas dwells at length on Luther's antisemitism. That discussion closes with his coined phrase '*simul justus et peccator*' (p.42): Christian were simultaneously justified before God (*simul justus*) and sinners (*et peccator*). Luther, though passionately antisemitic, was still great. He does not reflect on how someone could use such reasoning to sanctify any politician.

When a leader does right, the supporter could plead '*justus*'; when they do wrong, they can plead '*simul justus et peccator*'. God's politician, right or wrong.

Metaxas' chapter on Billy Graham is also insightful. Graham expressed remorse for overstepping his calling when commenting on political matters beyond his expertise (p.225). He also regretted 'diminish[ing] his evangelical impact and compromis[ing] his message' through involvement in partisan politics (p.234). More profoundly, Graham 'seemed to have forgotten at times that many people—including presidents—turn their best face to clergy and that politicians sometimes use religious figures for political ends' (p.229). These charges are routinely levelled at Trump's evangelical supporters (including Metaxas). Critics say the 'court evangelicals' are so close to Trump that they overestimate their expertise, fail to grasp the damage to their witness and do not perceive the extent to which Trump manipulates them.[52]

Michael L. Brown

Michael L. Brown describes himself as a Jewish believer in Jesus. He holds a PhD in Near Eastern Languages and Literatures (New York University). He is a popular author and radio host and has held visiting or adjunct positions at several prominent evangelical seminaries. He hosts a nationally syndicated talk show, *The Line of Fire*, and frequently contributes to websites like *The Christian Post*.

'While in prayer one morning in 2016, I sensed the Lord whisper to me, "Write a book on the fall and rise of America"'.[53] That book, *Saving a Sick America*, starts with a Rip Van Winkle-like account of a man who fell asleep on 7 June 1961 while watching *Leave It to Beaver* only to awake 'in hell' (present-day America). America entered that nightmare, Brown argues, and his book charts moral degradation across the centuries.

Brown's first chapter asks, 'How Good Were the Good Old Days?' He acknowledges that the 1960s were 'far from perfect' – noting how 'segregation was the law of the land, and women had far fewer opportunities than men, just to mention two of society's inequities'.[54] He pushes further back and details 'our major failings as a nation, including the practice of slavery and our treatment of the Native Americans'. Weighed against these failures is a 'steady Christian witness against slavery in our national history'.[55]

He tells one long, regressive story from colonial America through the Revolution and the 1960s and into the present.[56] American exceptionalism was built on biblical principles, and the loss of this foundation precipitated a national collapse.[57] He wants to restore America – but not in a theocratic mould or in a way that fails to respect diversity in modern America. The clock cannot be turned back. America needs revival, not legislation.[58]

In 2018, Brown published *Donald Trump is Not My Savior*. The book describes his evolving and uneasy decision to back Trump. He is keenly aware of the 'paradox' of evangelical support for the president, but Trump delivers justice for evangelicals.[59] MAGA is not primarily about recapturing America's 'biblical heritage'. The president and the average Protestant have separate (but complementary) jobs.[60] Evangelicals should expect great things from Trump, but they should not set their expectations of godliness too high.

Finally, Brown's *Jezebel's War With America* (2017) details a cosmic war stretching from the biblical past into the American present. The main characters are Jezebel ('the most wicked woman in the Bible') and Jehu (the morally lax king of Northern Israel who was nonetheless used by God in the defenestration and execution of Jezebel).[61] Building on the enormously influential prophetic word of the messianic rabbi Jonathan Cahn, Trump is a Jehu figure.[62] Lest the reader miss who might be the personification of evil, Brown asks 'Is Hillary Clinton a contemporary Jezebel?'[63] There is an arresting resonance between chants of 'Lock her up' (Clinton) and 'Cast her down' (Jezebel).

The prophets

If you walked into Barnes & Noble in early 2020, you might have found a dozen or more books that connect Donald Trump with biblical prophecy. I describe only a few of these prophecy 'experts' and prophets below.[64] In *Unholy*, Sarah Posner discusses the influence of this 'formidable spiritual army of self-styled prophets defending their own King Cyrus'.[65] She notes how many who write on Trump's evangelical supporters do not consider these people to be influential. However, in keeping with Trump's anti-elitism, he has elevated these marginal voices and allowed their prophetic words to inform policy.[66] I discuss these prophets as a collective – even though their denominational affiliations are quite diverse – since they form a chorus that sings of Trump's role in God's plan of bringing about the fulfilment of prophecy.[67]

Prophecy experts place the events of 2016 within an eschatological timeline drawn from Scripture. Some of these prophets go so far as to utter new prophecies. This cadre of prophets (often disagreeing among themselves) are energised by prophecies they believe have already been fulfilled. A significant percentage of these persons have had direct access to the president.

In their works, America's sins are often mentioned – but these are the sins championed by the Democrats (like abortion). Focused as they are on the future, these prophets rarely discuss anything negative in America's deep past (17th to mid-20th centuries). They are often more interested in linking Hebrew Bible exemplars and eschatological figures with America's present and future.

The televangelist John Hagee has a long history of prophetic writing (e.g. speculation over Blood Moons). His publications often support Israel, and he recently delivered the benediction at the opening of the American Embassy in Jerusalem. In a section of *Earth's Last Empire* titled 'Donald J. Trump – Making America Great Again', Hagee argued that restoring American greatness necessitates returning to the Reagan era – and Reagan was animated by the founding principles. 'The genetic code of the republic is also the genetic code of the Republican Party'.[68] 'If President Trump fails', he ominously warns, 'Make way for the New World Order!'[69] Hagee was not concerned with how the Old American Order was complicit in racism, sexism and exploitation.

Mark Taylor, a retired fighter, claims that God started talking to him in 2011 about Donald Trump's presidential victory. His prophecies were recently turned into a full-length film – produced in partnership with Liberty University. Taylor initially thought these prophetic words would be fulfilled in 2012.[70] 'Before Donald Trump swept the nation with the words "Make America Great Again", . . . God had already told me that He would bring greatness to us again. He told me that He had chosen Trump as His anointed, *for such a time as this*' [Esther 4:14].[71] Taylor said, 'God told me that He is choosing His dream team to run this country'.[72] His book is eschatologically hopeful – in contrast to others who foresee an imminent apocalypse. Lucifer and the New World Order will fall. The 'seeds' planted at the nation's 'beginning' will grow into an 'end-time harvest'.[73]

> America has, since the beginning, been a force for good within the modern world. This is a fact rarely acknowledged by our modern cynics. As humans, we sometimes get so hung up on burning America for her sins that we don't remember the sacrifices America has made for the good of others.[74]

One shouldn't dwell on America's historical failures because God will lead the nation to new vistas of greatness.[75]

One of the most influential prophets is Lance Wallnau, 'an evangelist whose popularity and visibility have skyrocketed in the Trump era', according to Sarah Posner.[76] Wallnau claims in *God's Chaos Candidate* (October 2016) that

> prior to my first meeting with Trump I heard the Lord say to me, 'Donald Trump is a wrecking ball to the spirit of political correctness!' I published this prophetic word right away, exactly as I heard it, at the beginning of the 2016 Primary Election season.[77]

The second revelation came before a second meeting with Trump. God impressed on him that the 45th president would be like the leader in Isaiah 45 – King Cyrus.[78] The progressive shadow government had already constructed the nation's future, but Cyrus came in like a wrecking ball. Wallnau divides American history into 'crucibles': (1) 1775–1783; (2) 1860–1865; (3) 1929–1945. 'The fourth crucible is upon us'.[79] Pilgrims and Puritans are not mentioned, and all the crucibles seem to relay crises from a white perspective. Wallnau labours to explain Trump's appeal to many African Americans (so Trump is not a racist). However, he nowhere seriously engages with America's history of racism, sexism and exploitation.

Alveda C. King, niece of Martin Luther King Jr., has long been a controversial public voice. Decline pervades her narrative in *America Return to God*. 'Even in the midst of all her problems of sin, racism, poverty, broken hearts and families, America once dreamed of a better tomorrow'.[80] She argues that 'repenting, rebuilding, repairing, restoring and returning to God here in America' is hindered by national unwillingness to face up to 'racism and the subsequent white privilege'.[81] Racism is bipartisan. She describes the racist origins of Planned Parenthood.[82] If the Right needs to confront the New Jim Crow, the Left needs to confront the new eugenics – abortion. She advocates 'Abolishing Slavery – Past and Present (Negro slaves, babies in the womb)'.[83] She also highlights the mistreatment of Native Americans.[84] Trump 'wanted to "make America great again". He speaks of "building a wall"'; King of restoring spiritual walls (patterned on Nehemiah). She repeats prophecies by Cahn and lends her support to the Trump-Cyrus connection advocated by Wallnau. In 2016, 'God has decided the outcome. "We the People" have voted in 2016, advancing a shift for the sanctity of life, family and community'.[85] Of the prophets discussed here, she speaks the most of historical and modern racism. Doubtless, her family history and her own experience of racism keep these aspects of American history at the forefront.

Finally, Stephen E. Strang is a prominent charismatic journalist with connections to the president. He has popularised the prophetic interpretations of Taylor, Cahn, Wallnau and Hagee (among others). *God and Trump* (foreword by Mike Huckabee) chronicles Strang's conversion to Trump. A thick sense of providence pervades, and he mentions miracles, prophecy and the belief that Trump is a Cyrus figure. The nation was built on Christian principles and led by those with a deep sense of divine mission. He does not mention much before the 1950s – a nearly idealised time. Of course, those under Jim Crow 'don't look back fondly on those days'.[86] *Trump Aftershock* (foreword by Jerry Falwell Jr.) continues this narrative as President Trump battles the Deep State. An appendix lists events in the president's '500 Days of American Greatness'.[87] *God, Trump and the 2020 Election* (foreword by Eric Metaxas) calls for continued support, proffers prophetic interpretations and explains what is at stake should Trump lose.[88] In a fourth book, *God, Trump, and COVID-19* (foreword by Lori Bakker), he argues that the pandemic heightened the need to support Trump, and the cadre of prophets have doubled down on their efforts.[89] In the first three works, Strang argued that Trump was the best choice for minorities. Although justice issues are important in the present, he does not dwell on the history of national wrongs.

Conclusion

What can be learned about the contours of historical memory from these Protestants who call for restored greatness? First, as the example of Os Guinness indicates, restoration need not lead to the sanctification of Trump. Most, however, see Trump as uniquely ordained by God to arrest American decline. Second, Protestant supporters of Trump are generally not using 'elite' Christian publishers (e.g. Baker, Eerdmans, IVP, Fortress). They reach large audiences through small and largely unknown publishing houses (e.g. FrontLine, Defender, Killer Sheep, Elijah List – although some use Thomas Nelson and Regnery). This complements Trump's anti-elitism. Third, most of their decline narratives begin in the 1950s or 1960s. Fourth, many of these authors mention America's historical failures concerning racism, sexism and exploitation. These confessions may surprise MAGA critics. However, their admissions are cursory and sometimes border on dismissal. They see little benefit in dwelling on the disreputable aspects of the past. Real American history is honourable, and even the failures highlight how great the country is. Some national sins (like slavery) are so heavy they will forever tip the scales, and it seems many on the Right bracket out America's weightiest failures when calculating greatness. These authors differ in their approach to MAGA, but they agree that the renewal of American greatness requires a return to God. Returning to God necessitates a recovery of what made America great between 1620 and the 1950s.

Notes

1 Tim Alberta, *American Carnage: On the Front Lines of the Republican Civil War and the Rise of President Trump* (New York: Harper, 2019), 260.

2 Danny Toma, *America First: Understanding the Trump Doctrine* (Washington, DC: Regnery, 2018), 4.
3 On these and other rulings, see Frances FitzGerald, *The Evangelicals: The Struggle to Shape America* (New York: Simon & Schuster, 2017).
4 Jones, *The End of White Christian America*, 51. Khyati Y. Joshi argues white Christianity, in particular white Protestantism, is still treated as the norm and favoured in court (*White Christian Privilege: The Illusion of Religious Equality in America* [New York: New York University Press, 2020]).
5 See a longer list of cases in Harry R. Jackson Jr. and Tony Perkins, *Personal Faith, Public Policy: The 7 Urgent Issues that We, as People of Faith, Need to Come Together and Solve* (Lake Mary, FL: FrontLine, 2008), 18–20.
6 Steven Waldman, *Sacred Liberty: America's Long, Bloody, and Ongoing Struggle for Religious Freedom* (New York: HarperOne, 2019), 199.
7 Trump, *Crippled America*, 132.
8 Posner, *Unholy*, xiii.
9 'White Evangelicals See Trump as Fighting for Their Beliefs, Though Many Have Mixed Feelings About His Personal Conduct' (12 Mar 2020). Online: www.pewforum.org/2020/03/12/white-evangelicals-see-trump-as-fighting-for-their-beliefs-though-many-have-mixed-feelings-about-his-personal-conduct/. Retrieved 23 June 2020.
10 David E. Fitch, *The Church of Us vs. Them: Freedom from a Faith That Feeds on Making Enemies* (Grand Rapids: Brazos, 2019), chap. 7. See also Katherine Stewart, *The Power Worshippers: Inside the Dangerous Rise of Religious Nationalism* (New York: Bloomsbury, 2020).
11 D. James Kennedy, *What If America Were a Christian Nation Again?* (Nashville: Thomas Nelson, 2003).
12 George Barna and David Barton, *U-Turn: Restoring America to the Strength of Its Roots* (Lake Mary, FL: FrontLine, 2014), 1, 5, 7.
13 For example, the evangelical theologian Wayne Grudem lists nine possible meanings behind the 'Christian nation' question. For five of the meanings, he answers 'yes'; for four he answers 'no'. He thinks the question is unhelpful (*Politics According to the Bible: A Comprehensive Resource for Understanding Modern Political Issues in Light of Scripture* [Grand Rapids: Zondervan, 2010], 64–5).
14 John Fea, *Believe Me: The Evangelical Road to Donald Trump* (Grand Rapids: Eerdmans, 2018), Kindle Loc. 2042–4; cf. idem., *Was America Founded as a Christian Nation? A Historical Introduction* (Rev. ed.; Louisville, KY: Westminster John Knox, 2016), chap. 1–3.
15 Khyati Y. Joshi, for example, argues that Christianity was assumed to be normative and given preferential treatment from the Founding (*White Christian Privilege*).
16 It is also true, as I read somewhere, that persecution inflation is as old as persecution. Perhaps inflation is related to denial.
17 For example, Jones, *Beyond the Messy Truth*, 25; John M. Perkins, *One Blood: Parting Words to the Church on Race and Love* (Chicago: Moody, 2018), 118–19.
18 Hochschild, *Strangers in Their Own Land*; Nancy Isenberg, *White Trash: The 400-Year Untold History of Class in America* (New York: Penguin, 2016); Robert Wuthnow, *The Left Behind: Decline and Rage in Rural America* (Princeton: Princeton University Press, 2018); Yael Tamir, *Why Nationalism* (Princeton:

Princeton University Press, 2019); R. R. Reno, *Return of the Strong Gods: Nationalism, Populism, and the Future of the West* (Washington, DC: Regnery Gateway, 2019); see also J. D. Vance, *Hillbilly Elegy: A Memoir of a Family and Culture in Crisis* (New York: Harper Collins, 2016). One of the strengths of interview-based books like Ben Bradlee Jr.'s account of how a democratic stronghold in Pennsylvania (Luzerne County) swung decidedly for Trump in 2016 is that he shows how MAGA meant different things to different supporters (*The Forgotten: How the People of One Pennsylvania County Elected Donald Trump and Changed America* [New York: Little, Brown and Company, 2018]). See also Ken Stern, *Republican Like Me: How I Left the Liberal Bubble and Learned to Love the Right* (New York: Harper Collins, 2017).

19 Hart, *Trump and Us*, 5.
20 And many on the Right argue that Trump haters are trying to fundamentally alter the nation in their quest to derail his agenda. See, for example, Kimberly Strassel, *Resistance (At All Costs): How Trump Haters Are Breaking America* (New York: Twelve, 2019).
21 Hart, *Trump and Us*, 118.
22 Ibid., 98.
23 Donald J. Trump, 'Remarks by President Trump at the National Day of Prayer Event and Signing of the Executive Order on Promoting Free Speech and Religious Liberty' (4 May 2017). Online: www.whitehouse.gov/briefings-statements/remarks-president-trump-national-day-prayer-event-signing-executive-order-promoting-free-speech-religious-liberty/. Retrieved 31 Mar 2020.
24 Fea, *Believe Me*, chap. 4.
25 Robert Jeffress, *Twilight's Last Gleaming: How America's Last Days Can Be Your Best Days* (Brentwood, TN: Worthy, 2011). The Huckabee quote is from the introduction.
26 Robert Jeffress, *Praying for America: 40 Inspiring Stories and Prayers for Our Nation* (New York: FaithWords, 2020), 94, 96.
27 Cal Thomas, *America's Expiration Date: The Fall of Empires and Superpowers . . . and the Future of the United States* (Grand Rapids: Zondervan, 2020), 9.
28 Ibid., 11.
29 Ibid., 139.
30 Ibid., 140.
31 Ibid., 145.
32 Ibid., 146.
33 Os Guinness, *Last Call for Liberty: How America's Genius for Freedom Has Become Its Greatest Threat* (Downers Grove: InterVarsity, 2018), 8.
34 Ibid., 5.
35 Ibid., 61.
36 Ibid., 44; cf. 45, 212, 283.
37 Ibid., 280–1.
38 Ibid., 281.
39 Ibid., 46.
40 Eric Metaxas, *If You Can Keep It: The Forgotten Promise of American Liberty* (New York: Penguin, 2016), 51–77.
41 Ibid., 6–7, 21–4, 212–17.
42 Ibid., 229.
43 Ibid., 116.

44 Ibid., 119.
45 Ibid., 121.
46 Ibid., 226–7.
47 Ibid., 229, 231.
48 Ibid., 75–114.
49 Thomas S. Kidd, *America's Religious History: Faith, Politics, and the Shaping of a Nation* (Grand Rapids: Zondervan, 2019), 40. Metaxas's new book briefly mentions Whitefield and slavery but in a dismissive way (*Seven More Men: And the Secret of their Greatness* [Grand Rapids: Zondervan, 2020], 11, 68).
50 Amy Gutmann, Wendell Pritchett and Craig Carnaroli, 'Penn Announces Plans to Remove Statue of George Whitefield and Forms Working Group to Study Campus Names and Iconography' (2 July 2020). Online: https://penntoday.upenn.edu/announcements/penn-announces-plans-remove-statue-george-whitefield-and-forms-working-group-study. Retrieved 12 July 2020.
51 Metaxas, *If You Can Keep It*, 208–29.
52 Stewart, *The Power Worshippers*.
53 Brown, *Saving a Sick America*, xvi.
54 Ibid., 7.
55 Ibid., 27.
56 Ibid., 13.
57 Ibid., 27.
58 Ibid., 38–9.
59 Michael L. Brown, *Donald Trump Is Not My Savior: An Evangelical Leader Speaks His Mind About the Man He Supports as President* (Shippensburg, PA: Destiny Image, 2018), 323.
60 Ibid., 22.
61 Michael L. Brown, *Jezebel's War With America: The Plot to Destroy Our Country and What We Can Do to Turn the Tide* (Lake Mary, FL: FrontLine, 2019), 3. Originally published in 2017.
62 Ibid., 153. See Jonathan Cahn, *The Paradigm: The Ancient Blueprint that Holds the Mystery of Our Times* (Lake Mary, FL: FrontLine, 2017), 226.
63 Brown, *Jezebel's War With America*, 150.
64 See also works by Jonathan Chan, Jeremiah Johnson, Robert Henderson, Thomas R. Horn, Paul McGuire and Troy Anderson, Larry Sparks, Bob Thiel, John Whitman and Smith Wigglesworth. Many of these persons are associated with Jim Bakker. Additionally, a book by Trump's personal campaign photographer ends with a discussion of 'Apocalypse: ἀποκάλυψις' and the signs that God is fulfilling prophecy through Trump (Gene Ho, *TRUMPography: How Biblical Principles Paved the Way to the American President* [Bloomington, IN: iUniverse, 2018], 161–8).
65 Posner, *Unholy*, 52.
66 Ibid., 247.
67 Several come from the more Charismatic end of the spectrum, and some are part of the New Apostolic Reformation – a relatively new movement that believes in direct revelation. Some are involved in POTUS Shield, a network of prayer warriors who defend Trump. This ethnically diverse group includes military leaders like General Jerry Boykin.
68 John Hagee, *Earth's Last Empire: The Final Game of Thrones* (Franklin, TN: Worthy, 2018), 211.
69 Ibid., 215.

70 Mark Taylor, *The Trump Prophecies: The Astonishing True Story of the Man Who Saw Tomorrow . . . and What He Says Is Coming Next* (Rev. ed.; Crane, MO: Defender, 2019), 4–5.
71 Ibid., 57.
72 Ibid., 161.
73 Ibid., 95–6.
74 Ibid., 104.
75 Ibid., 111–13.
76 Posner, *Unholy*, 31.
77 Lance Wallnau, *God's Chaos Candidate: Donald J. Trump and the American Unraveling* (Keller, TX: Killer Sheep Media, 2016), 21.
78 Ibid., 22–5.
79 Ibid., 14–15.
80 Alveda C. King, *America Return to God: Repent from Sin, Rebuild the Wall, Repair the Gates, Restore the Dream* (Albany, NY: Elijah List, 2016), 35.
81 Ibid., 59.
82 Ibid., 63.
83 Ibid., 66; cf. 103–9. On the debated link between slavey and abortion, see Justin Buckley Dyer, *Slavery, Abortion, and the Politics of Constitutional Meaning* (Cambridge: Cambridge University Press, 2013), 28.
84 King, *America Return to God*, 66–7.
85 Ibid., 151.
86 Stephen E. Strang, *God and Donald Trump* (Lake Mary, FL: FrontLine, 2018), 15.
87 Strang, *Trump Aftershock*, 229–34. See a similar list at the back of Reed, *God and Country*.
88 Stephen E. Strang, *God, Trump and the 2020 Election: Why He Must Win and What's at Stake If He Loses* (Lake Mary, FL: FrontLine, 2018).
89 Stephen E. Strang, *God, Trump, and COVID-19: How the Pandemic Is Affecting Christians, the World, and America's 2020 Election* (Lake Mary, FL: FrontLine, 2020).

4 Make America lament

The burden of memory

MAGA Protestants often treat the Bible as 'the Forrest Gump of history', as Katherine Stewart puts it in *The Power Worshipers*. 'Whenever something big is happening, the Bible is there, and always doing good'.[1] Many in the *Make America Lament* crowd might also view the Bible as ubiquitous in American history, but they would not say it was 'always doing good'.

During the Obama administration, the conservative Right told decline narratives.[2] Movements like the Tea Party mined the past for resources and inspiration for the present. Now, under Trump, the Left has set its hand to the plough of historical reflection. Henry A. Giroux, a professor and cultural critic based at McMaster University, said it is now 'crucial' to have a 'revival of historical memory as a central political strategy'.[3]

Many Protestants do not pine for a political or religious golden age, for they argue it never existed. Further, past injustice is too continuous with present injustice. Consider these words by Drew G. I. Hart (Assistant Professor of Theology at Messiah University) in *Trouble I've Seen: Changing the Way the Church Views Racism*:

> We have yet to admit that everything that happens in the present is merely the unfolding of America's birth: stolen land and conquest, genocide of Native Americans, stolen labor from African people, and the development of a dehumanizing antiblack ideology.[4]

The burden of memory is eased by fellow travellers throughout history who resisted the tide of oppression. Of particular importance are preachers, professors, politicians, activists, musicians, playwrights, poets, novelists and artists who pushed against racism, sexism and exploitation.

Large portions of Scripture focus on lament. However, many white American churches have little room for communal lamentation in their theology, preaching and singing. In contrast, the African American church, in particular, has long harnessed communal lament as a source of strength. Those who want to *Make America Lament*, generally speaking, do not want to humiliate, alienate or punish whites. Yes, an honest look at America's past and present will be painful. However, the call for lament is an invitation to intimacy. Latasha Morrison describes the process whereby members of 'Bridge groups' are led 'out of denial and ignorance, into lamentation, and ultimately into racial solidarity. . . . Acknowledgement should lead us towards lament, toward seeking mercy, toward a collective conviction that we can and must do better'.[5] The one called into lament is not left outside. They are brought near, closer to the vulnerability, hurt and anger that are the product of historical injustice.

Those who want to *Make America Lament* are burdened by different memories. Although many grieve moral decline since the 1950s, they tend to focus on the personal and structural racism found down every avenue of American history. These Protestants may say with Frederick Douglass that presumptions of 'national greatness' should be met with 'a fiery stream of biting ridicule, blasting reproach, withering sarcasm, and stern rebuke'.[6] Although the following brief history focuses on the African American experience, many calling for lament also link this struggle with the fight for ever-widening equality in every sphere of life.

The enslavement of African persons in the English colonies predates Plymouth. Settlers became dependent on African and American Indian enslaved persons from early on – replacing indentured servitude (in which whites were also bound) with race-based, heritable chattel slavery.[7] A long history of exclusion from rights and privileges followed. Ongoing racism was not a bug of the America system but a feature – and this feature operated with ruthless efficiency throughout the nation's history.

At a deeper level, many white accounts of history confuse the opposition to slavery with the advocacy of equality. All who advocated racial equality wanted to abolish slavery; only a fraction of those who wanted abolition desired the equality of the races. Abraham Lincoln is a good example. Throughout his political career, he argued that slavery was wrong. However, he resolutely argued against equality with blacks, believing them inferior and shuddering at the thought of intermarriage.[8] Confusing abolitionism with anti-racism masks ongoing racism from the 1860s to the present.

The ignorance of white Americans is also a burden. 'Our only chance at dismantling racial injustice', writes Austin Channing Brown in *I'm Still Here: Black Dignity in a World Made for Whiteness,* 'is being more curious about its origin than we are worried about our comfort'.[9] There is an urgency to her writing since she can feel 'the distance between history and myself collapsing'.[10]

Forgetting the past was not accidental. In *The Cross and the Lynching Tree*, the eminent theologian of Black Liberation, James H. Cone, said the following: 'Many white religious leaders, scholars and churches have done everything they can to forget the vigilante violence unleashed on African Americans'.[11]

Whites need to learn history. Consider this admission by Pastor Daniel Hill in *White Awake* who says that until his late twenties 'I certainly had no in-depth knowledge of the history of lynching, nor could I comprehend how the terror of that period left aftershocks in the black community that have been felt for decades'.[12] He argues that many whites have significant gaps in their understanding of American history.[13]

Perhaps the largest gap in white memory stretches from the end of slavery to the Civil Rights Movement. Broadly speaking, white accounts tend to write minorities out of the story, sanitise many unflattering elements or weave an optimistic tale out of the tattered strands of racism. Whites look fondly at the Civil War that secured freedom for enslaved persons. However, many are not well acquainted with the successful efforts to carry on aspects of slavery under other names – particularly through the loss of voting rights, the convict lease system and the 1896 'separate but equal' decision (*Plessy v. Ferguson*). It is in this forgotten century that the black and brown body went from being associated with biological inferiority to being more associated with criminality.

Jim Crow laws are more widely known by white Americans, but they are often disconnected from present racism. Historical racism in the North is seldom talked about, in part because the North likes to remind itself that it was on the right side of the slavery debate. After slavery, increasing terror in the South fed northward migration and contributed to growing anger among northern whites.[14] Once in the North, redlining and racially restricted housing covenants pushed minorities into impoverished communities and then trapped them there.[15]

Particularly in the South, the forced integration of the public school system led many Christians to form segregated private schools. White supremacy wrapped its tendrils around religious liberty. Anger over *Brown v. Board of Education* and its aftermath, not primarily *Roe v. Wade*, turned conservative Christians into a political force. As Jim Crow ended, racial prejudice morphed – most notably into a system of mass incarceration that adversely impacts minorities.[16] To add insult to injury, there are ongoing attempts to restrict voting rights – and these efforts have deep historical roots.[17] Economic disparities, too, continue to increase.

The past, in hundreds of big and small ways, influences the present. Whether in theology, ethics, politics or culture, the white perspective is assumed as normative. Further, the English language often perpetuates damaging views about skin colour through the association of 'white' with good or pure and 'black' or 'brown' with bad or defiled. Racism seems as inescapable as the English language.

Richard T. Hughes, Distinguished Professor of Religion at Messiah University, has worked for decades on the narratives that Americans tell themselves about their past. The first edition of *Myths America Lives By* (2003) explored five myths. They are the myth of (1) the chosen nation, (2) nature's nation (America's ideals are rooted in nature), (3) the millennial nation (America ushers in a golden age), (4) the Christian nation and (5) the innocent nation. By the time of the second edition in 2018, he had become convinced of another myth, indeed the most important one:

> The fundamental argument of this book [in its second edition], therefore, is twofold – first, that the Myth of White Supremacy is the primal American myth that informs all the others and, second, that one of the chief functions of the other five myths is to protect and obscure the Myth of White Supremacy, to hide it from our awareness, and to assure us that we remain innocent after all.[18]

These attitudes, he argues, are often unconscious – but that does not make them less perilous or potent. Make America Great Again is a thinly coded version of Make America White Again.[19]

White churches are often silent about issues of justice that concern their minority sisters and brothers in Christ. Churches largely remain divided along ethnic and political lines. Whereas many white Christians claim they are not racist, and on a personal level have high opinions of minorities, they often advocate political policies that hurt minorities.[20]

The Obama presidency, for many, awakened hope that the United States turned a page on racism (the colour blind or post-racial society). Most Americans who opposed his policies were still proud the nation elected an African American to the presidency.[21] There were many promising signs that the nation was acknowledging its past and working towards reconciliation.

The writing, however, was on the wall: the birther controversy, racist signs at Tea Party rallies, the refusal to accept Obama's American or Christian credentials,[22] to name a few. Avowedly white supremacist groups were becoming more visible and vocal, and the growing Alt-Right movement prided itself on countering politically correct censorship with racially inflammatory language.

Many viewed these trends as a backlash against liberal modernity; others noted how white rage was closely linked with black advancement.[23] A rising awareness of police shootings of unarmed minorities, coupled with the 2015 massacre of African American worshipers in Charleston, propelled many into the streets to protest systemic injustice. Present injustice amplified past wrongs, leading the Rev. Dr William J. Barber II to call for a 'third reconstruction'.[24] Trump announced his candidacy the day before the

Charleston massacre, and the events of the following day underscored the sense that he was not the right person to heal racial wounds.

Among opponents of the president, there is widespread agreement about one thing: 'hats that say "Make America Great Again" . . . really means "Make America White Again"'.[25] Trump's election was widely seen as an angry white reaction to President Obama's person and policies – a 'whitelash', as Van Jones called it on election night.[26] Trump's presidency brought more evidence that MAGA was coded language for white supremacy, as Rev. Dr Kelly Brown Douglas argued after the killings of Breonna Taylor, Ahmaud Arbery and George Floyd.[27]

The burden of memory would not be so great if alleviation seemed forthcoming. Rather than laying aside the weights of centuries of racism, white America piled injustice on injury. Michelle Alexander's recent preface to *The New Jim Crow* passionately argues that MAGA restores many of the worst aspects of history: 'It can no longer be denied that the colorblind veneer of early twenty-first-century American democracy was just that: a veneer. Right beneath the surface lay an ugly reality that many Americans were not prepared to face'.[28] Alexander has seen enough of the president's rhetoric and actions to know where the MAGA time machine is headed. Although the president denies racism, this does not convince critics. 'Denial is the heartbeat of racism', writes Ibram X. Kendi in *How to Be an Antiracist*, 'beating across ideologies, races, and nations'.[29]

The change in national mood from 2008 to 2016 seems abrupt. 'We inhabit a backlash moment in American history of uncertain duration', writes Joseph J. Ellis in *American Dialogue*.[30] Only some of the causes of this backlash are racial. However, the racial element is likely to remain important: 'We should expect a major backlash to wash over us as we approach the middle of this century. . . . In or about 2045, the white population will become a statistical minority'.[31] MAGA, Ellis claims, is a foretaste of what is to come, and he hopes Americans will turn to their history to learn how to dialogue through difference.

Anxiety about the upcoming demography shift must be interpreted in light of academic and activist theories about race (an intricate language that the conservative media routinely strips of nuance and then weaponises). Whites know their numbers are declining; they also hear calls for whites to renounce whiteness or crucify whiteness – and they may have even heard that a professor said he wanted white genocide for Christmas.[32] Many conservative whites do not have the resources or time – let alone the will – to start understanding the academic theory behind this language. All they hear is that a growing minority wants to destroy white culture, history and even skin colour.

These statements feel like *macro*aggressions, and the Left often rewards those who are the most aggressive with this language. (The intricate language of *micro*aggressions is another discourse with which many conservative whites feel bludgeoned but often do not have the resources, time or will to understand.) Conservative whites react viscerally to the language of dismantling whiteness. The Left often takes this reaction as a confirmation that they hit the right nerve and should double down on the linguistic incision. Conservative whites, however, worry the Left wants to cut an artery. As an act of communication, the language critiquing racism often fails to reach its target audience.

There is a great challenge ahead in the decades leading to this demography shift: To help white Americans learn the history of racism, confront injustice in the present and welcome the growing diversity – and to do this in a manner that does not stoke fears, confirm prejudices or make whites feel embattled.

Just as *Make America Great Again* Protestants turned to history to chart America's path forward, those who desire to *Make America Lament* are eager to discuss the past. What they choose to remember differs starkly from the optimistic and patriotic narratives of America's past that were discussed earlier.

Sheri Faye Rosendahl

Sheri Faye Rosendahl is an author and blogger at *Patheos.com* who writes on issues of justice and oppression – particularly related to refugees. Her writing is unashamedly confrontational – particularly when writing on conservative Christianity and politics. As a white American, Rosendahl's *Not Your White Jesus* advocates for the oppressed by emphasising that the 'non-white Jesus' was a refugee.

> Jesus is not a white guy. . . . Jesus isn't American; he's not even campaigning for America's greatness! There's more. He actually doesn't care more about Americans than any other humans in the entire world (including Muslims and Communists).[33]

American greatness infects the church and leads to a devaluing of life at home and abroad.

For Rosendahl, these misconceptions are deeply rooted in a troubling American past: '[T]he ways of Jesus are pretty hard to align with an ideology that sees America as our God-given promised land (well, after we wiped out the natives in the name of Jesus)'.[34] American injustice and hubris move in tandem.

> This idea of America as a 'city on a hill' dates back to 1630, when John Winthrop envisioned the Puritan colony as a light to the nations. And

> maybe we are a light on a hill – a light that ends up starting a forest fire that destroys the rest of the world. When we see a church choir sing a 'Make America Great Again' song, proclaiming Donald Trump's signature slogan as an act of worship, we have passed into the realm of a nationalistic cult obsession.[35]

She disfigures Winthrop's phrase that is routinely used by Democrats and Republicans to argue for American greatness.[36] In a blog post on Christian nationalists' claims to greatness, she asks why would 'any decent humans be proud of these sorts of American ideals?'[37] From the arrival of Europeans to the present, she tells one continuous story of shame.

Rosendahl worries that the refugee Jesus is lost *again* to nationalism. 'Americans' desire for (reclaimed?) greatness isn't unique. Jesus' contemporaries wanted to make Israel great again'.[38] The confusion about Christ that led to his crucifixion continues to lead Christians astray. To become more Christian, Christians must become less American.

Cornel West

Cornel West is a prominent author, activist and public intellectual and is Professor of the Practice of Public Philosophy at Harvard. In the introduction to *The Cornel West Reader*, he said, 'Three related and fundamental questions motivate my writings: What does it mean to be *human*? What does it mean to be *modern*? What does it mean to be *American*?' Informing all of these pursuits is the attempt to

> bank his all on radical – not rational – choice and on the courage to love enacted by a particular Palestinian Jew named Jesus, who was crucified by the powers that be, betrayed by cowardly comrades and misconstrued by corrupt churches that persist, and yet is remembered by those of us terrified and mesmerized by the impossible possibility of his love.

To be American is to grapple with open-ended debate, to experiment with democracy, to forever keep the concerns of the marginalised in sight and 'to downplay history in the name of hope, to ignore memory in the cause of possibility'. He does not mean forgetting America's history of injustice, for remembering those sordid chapters is integral to progress. However, where America has been should not constrain where it is going.[39]

West has not published any monographs since the run-up to the 2016 election. He has, however, edited or contributed to several volumes. His anthology *The Radical King* argued that Americans needed to encounter (some for the first time) Martin Luther King Jr.'s unsettling prophetic message. He worried that King has been 'Santa-Clausified – tamed, domesticated, sanitized, and sterilized'.[40] History has that effect. By admiring – but not really hearing – King, white Americans can continue on their merry way thinking their nation is not structurally racist.

His concerns are with the present and the future, but he also wants America to confront its deep past. In the new introduction to *Race Matters*, he described the conditions that made America possible:

> And the revolutionary American effort was built on Indigenous peoples' land and bodies, as well as on Black peoples' enslavement and expropriation. In short, imperial expansion, predatory capitalism, and white supremacy were the driving background conditions for the possibility of the precious democratic idea and its practice in America.[41]

America gained the world but lost its soul, if it ever had a soul to begin with. Seen against this history, Trump 'is as American as apple pie. Yet he is a sign of our spiritual bankruptcy'.[42] He is a symptom, not the cause, of the present crisis.

Michael Eric Dyson

Rev. Michael Eric Dyson is Professor of Sociology at Georgetown University. *Tears We Cannot Stop: A Sermon to White America* (2017) harnesses the heartbreak from recent police shootings to plead with white Americans (his 'beloved'). He wants them to feel with minorities and fit modern injustice into America's larger story. 'White denial thrives on shifts and pivots. "It was my ancestors, not me, who did this to you". But what looks like confession is really denial'.[43] He uses Toni Morrison's

> 'rememory' and 'disremembering' to help us to think about who, or what, the nation chooses to remember or forget. President Donald Trump chose 'Make America Great Again' as his 2016 campaign slogan. It sounded the call to white America to return to simpler, better days. But the golden age of the past is a fiction, a projection of nostalgia that selects what is most comforting to remember.[44]

This past was

> not great for all; in fact, it is a past that was not great at all, not with racism and sexism clouding the culture. Going back to a time that was great depends on deliberate disremembering. One of the great perks of being white in America is the capacity to forget at will. . . . Beloved,

you must admit that the denial of fact, indeed denial as fact, has shaped your version of American history.[45]

America was never great; how could it be with the millstone of racism and sexism around its neck? By looking back with courage and honesty, white Americans can begin to address these enduring sins.

In *What Truth Sounds Like*, Dyson repeatedly pulls white Americans into a confrontation with the past. 'Trump and the white bigotocracy have little patience for real history', he writes. They think African Americans have 'pimped' slavery and 'lived too long on the memory of something that happened so long ago that it can't possibly have anything to do with what's going on today'.[46] This 'bigotocracy is angry that slavery is seen as this nation's original sin'.[47] Dyson's solution is simple and elegantly worded: 'America could only purge its hateful bigotry if it confronted its past with the same energy it embraced its founding fathers and celebrated the myth of American individualism'.[48]

Jemar Tisby

Jemar Tisby serves as the president of The Witness. He is a graduate of Notre Dame and Reformed Theological Seminary and is pursuing a history PhD at the University of Mississippi. After the killing of George Floyd, Tisby's book from 2019, *The Color of Compromise*, rocketed onto *The New York Times*'s bestseller lists. The book opens with a foreword by the popular hip-hop artist Lecrae, who recently felt thrown under the bus by white evangelicals who objected when he pointed out historical racism. Just as Christians cannot pick and choose the parts of the Bible they like, Lecrae wrote, 'We either fully acknowledge the entire history [of America] or dismiss it all'.[49]

Tisby wants to convince the American church of complicity in racism. However, 'Given the history, *complicity* is a weak word'. The church was not carried along by racist tides; 'white Christians have often been the current, whipping racism into waves of conflict that rock and divide the people of God'.[50] Self-congratulatory stories come easy to American Christians, 'but honestly recognizing their failures and inconsistencies, especially when it comes to racism, remains an issue'.[51] He thinks that 'most Christians in America don't know how bad racism really is, so they don't respond with the necessary urgency'.[52]

Tisby notes something many analyses of racism in America overlook: 'nothing about American racism was inevitable. There was a period, from about 1500 to 1700, when race did not predetermine one's station and worth in society'.[53] Christians played an important role in the creation of racial hierarchies. 'But if racism can be made, it can be unmade'.[54]

The Color of Compromise spans American history. 'Christian complicity with racism in the twenty-first century looks different than complicity with racism in the past'.[55] Racism became more subtle and sophisticated. Christians should recognise that 'Trump traffics in harmful racial stereotypes'.[56] Instead, many Christians cared only about what Trump could offer. 'In the conservative Christian political mind, Trump, despite his [racism], promised to "Make Evangelicals Great Again"'.[57] As in previous centuries, American whites abandoned courageous Christianity and opted for power, ease, wealth and security.

Tisby's book aims at godly grief – and grief is closely related to lament.[58] Movements like Black Lives Matter give white Christians the opportunity to grieve with their neighbours.[59] And lament is one thing 'the American church can learn from the black church'.[60]

Mark Charles and Soong-Chan Rah

Make America lament. From beginning to end, this is the argument of *Unsettling Truths: The Ongoing, Dehumanizing Legacy of the Doctrine of Discovery*. Mark Charles is the son of a Navajo father and an American mother of Dutch heritage. He is an activist and 2020 Independent presidential candidate. Soong-Chan Rah immigrated from South Korea when he was a child. He is Professor of Church Growth and Evangelism at North Park University. Their book counts the cost of theological heresy on Indigenous populations.

The American church, like the nation, sees itself as exceptional, and high self-regard distorted the gospel and devalued life. Instead of 'confronting sinful racist perspectives theology becomes the tool of ongoing oppression'.[61] America's past is celebrated everywhere. Lament is absent, and with lament went truth. 'The absence of truth has resulted in the presence of injustice'.[62]

Their history aims at '*racial conciliation*', not '*racial reconciliation*', because the former 'implies a preexisting harmony and unity'.[63] 'Our country does not have a common memory', further problematising conciliation.[64] They write out of a love for white America and the white church. Centuries of injustice traumatised whites, and this trauma manifests itself in denial. 'The necessary corrective for this trauma is offered in the healing power of lament'.[65]

Europeans used the Doctrine of Discovery to confiscate lands and dominate bodies. Those who established a new Promised Land soon found Canaanites to kill. 'Winthrop's assertion of a special status for the Puritans in the New World justified the resulting genocide of the existing population in the American continent'.[66] Then the Constitution intentionally enshrined inequality.[67] Even the giants of American history must be remembered correctly: Lincoln, for example, did not truly believe black or native lives mattered.[68]

Inequality pervaded every aspect of American history: Women, Native Americans and African Americans were not given voting rights; Jim Crow laws abounded;

> Lynching, Indian removal, internment camps, segregation, and mass incarceration of people of color – all these and more – took place after the Fourteenth Amendment. And in 1970 the Fourteenth Amendment was used in Roe v. Wade, which concluded unborn babies are not human enough to be considered a person by the Constitution and therefore could be aborted.[69]

Americans are exceptionally good at defining away human rights.

Both Hillary Clinton (implicit) and Donald Trump (explicit) are spokespersons for American exceptionalism and for the continued dominance of whites.[70] Natives are routinely excluded from national decisions. For example, there can be 'no integrity' in immigration reform that excludes the original inhabitants of America.[71]

Because America has 'never lost a war that mattered', the nation has never been forced to rewrite history. Narratives of exceptionalism thrive in this environment. 'While this situation may sound like a blessing, never losing a war can be incredibly dangerous'.[72] America flatters itself that it is morally superior to Nazi Germany, but it is better only at winning wars.[73] Christians should not be concerned with restoring American greatness. Nor should the fight be to '"make the nation Christian again". . . . [T]hat is precisely what caused our problems in the first place'.[74] The empire-serving church needs to recognise it departed from Christ. A true understanding of history leads to lament, and lament opens up the doorway to racial conciliation.

Jonathan Walton

At the end of *Twelve Lies That Hold America Captive*, Jonathan Walton emphasises his desire for the book: 'My hope is that you would lament, confess, repent, and be blessed into the ministry of reconciliation'.[75] The book, up to that point, explained how distorted theology produced a damnable history and then went about covering up the crime. Walton is a minority who identifies with several racial and cultural groups. He is a graduate of Columbia University who works as an area ministry director for InterVarsity Christian Fellowship, where he focuses on human trafficking.

Walton notes how Obama's presidency raised his hopes, 'But then the American = white = male = Christian forcefully reasserted itself'.[76] In the context of resurgent white Christian nationalism, he notes how 'Make America Great Again resonates so strongly with one demographic but confuses and frightens others'.[77]

Many argue that a renewed unity is the answer to America's present division. Walton argues that 'we are the divided states of America in a united state of amnesia, choosing not to remember what's happened to pursue the unity we crave'.[78] Unity must be built on accurate history.

America must confront its past. This confrontation involves reevaluating figures from Christopher Columbus to John Winthrop to Jonathan Edwards. The admirable aspects of such persons cannot be divorced from their treatment of minorities.[79] He details historical injustice and enshrined inequality from 1790 to the New Jim Crow.[80] In contrast to the kingdom of God,

> The United States is rooted in genocide, land theft, institutionalized slave labor, and sexual exploitation. . . . There are great promises and aspirations in the US Constitution, but it is neither a holy text nor does it describe the plan of God for the renewal of all creation and the restoration of shalom.[81]

He insists that the United States is not the kingdom of God, and the two must remain distinguished.[82]

America's founding ideals were custom-built for white supremacy, and it is difficult to repurpose them.

> In present-day America, to take the Constitution and extrapolate equal value for every person is like putting a brand-new paint job, tinted windows, and fresh tires on a car with no engine or seats. It looks great on the outside but was never meant to move forward or carry anyone.[83]

Treating historical persons and documents as beyond reproach perpetuates the injustice that those individuals signed into law.

Walton dethrones the deified nation so that people can humble themselves before God and seek his kingdom. Only Christ can bear the weight of supremacy.[84] 'Lament, confession, repentance, and reconciliation are four steps in responding to suffering and seeking justice with Christ at the center'.[85]

Jonathan Wilson-Hartgrove

Jonathan Wilson-Hartgrove is a graduate of Eastern University and Duke Divinity School. In addition to writing, speaking and organising for justice, he works to provide a community for the formerly homeless and is a white minister at a historically black church in Durham, North Carolina.

In *Reconstructing the Gospel* (foreword by William J. Barber II), Wilson-Hartgrove argues the gospel was 'twisted to accommodate America's original sin', and it will remain twisted unless 'Christians in America . . . come to terms with how *institutional racism* has infected us'.[86] He calls this distorted faith 'slaveholder religion'.[87] Despite the prevalence of the distortion – or likely because of it – Americans do not remember racism in the past or recognise it in the present.

Trump's selective nostalgia perpetuates what is worst in American history. Worse yet, it ignores a shameful history that is already out in the open:

> Our missionaries were on the slave ships; our endowments were built up by stolen labor. We split denominations to support the Confederacy, blessed a violent Redemption movement [against Reconstruction], defended Jim Crow, fretted that civil rights preachers had forsaken their 'spiritual' calling, and cooperated in the criminalization of color, all the while exporting our religion with zeal.[88]

America's failings were 'Not just in the past. And not just in the South'.[89]

In *Revolution of Values*, he critiqued those who latch on to Trump and his slogan in a desire to preserve white dominance.[90] The real threat to American culture and Christianity is not 'progressive values' but 'the genocidal white supremacy and patriarchy that have compromised Christian witness throughout US history'.[91]

Conclusion

This chapter began with a very different burden of memories. *Make America Lament* Protestants sometimes speak of progress, but they emphasise an alarming continuity across the centuries. Part of confronting and overcoming this legacy is constantly remembering the theft of land from American Indians, the accumulation of wealth on the backs of African Americans and the marginalisation of women throughout history. Ahistorical 'greatness' facilitates injustice.

Make America Lament Protestants worry that MAGA is a call to restore the worst aspects of American history. The authors seem allergic to speaking fondly about America's past, and this is likely the case for one important reason: Although some may admire aspects of the American past, they seem to worry that patriotic appeals might short-circuit repentance and restitution. Like those discussed in the next chapter, they also want to make America *better*. However, they work for this goal by keeping the focus on America's lamentable past.

Notes

1. Stewart, *The Power Worshippers*, 137.
2. For example, Barna and Barton, *U-Turn*.
3. Henry A. Giroux, 'Trump's War on Dangerous Memory and Critical Thought', in Haki R. Madhubuti and Lasana Kazembe (eds.), *Not Our President: New Directions from the Pushed Out, the Others, and the Clear Majority in Trump's Stolen America* (No Place: Third World Press Foundation, 2017), 44 (41–52).
4. Drew G. I. Hart, *Trouble I've Seen: Changing the Way the Church Views Racism* (Harrisonburg, VA: Herald, 2016), 179.
5. Latasha Morrison, *Be the Bridge: Pursuing God's Heart for Racial Reconciliation* (Colorado Springs: WaterBrook, 2019), 29, 46.
6. Frederick Douglass, 'What to the Slave Is the Fourth of July' (5 June 1852), in Sherrow O. Pinder (ed.), *Black Political Thought: From David Walker to the Present* (Cambridge: Cambridge University Press, 2020), 40–4 (43).
7. Ibram X. Kendi, *Stamped from the Beginning: The Definitive History of Racist Ideas in America* (New York: Nation, 2016); Margaret Ellen Newell, *Brethren By Nature: New England Indians, Colonists, and the Origins of American Slavery* (Ithaca: Cornell University Press, 2015); Andrés Reséndez, *The Other Slavery: The Uncovered Story of Indian Enslavement in America* (Boston: Houghton Mifflin Harcourt, 2016); Wendy Warren, *New England Bound: Slavery and Colonization in Early America* (London: Liveright, 2016). On the history of white slavery, see Michael Guasco, *Slaves and Englishmen: Human Bondage in the Early Modern Atlantic World* (Philadelphia: University of Pennsylvania Press, 2014).
8. Terence Ball (ed.), *Lincoln: Political Writings and Speeches* (Cambridge: Cambridge University Press, 2013) 25, 48, 69, 143, 228–9.
9. Austin Channing Brown, *I'm Still Here: Black Dignity in a World Made for Whiteness* (New York: Convergent, 2018), 117.
10. Ibid., 58–9, cf. 152.
11. James H. Cone, *The Cross and the Lynching Tree* (Maryknoll, NY: Orbis, 2011), 165.
12. Daniel Hill, *White Awake: An Honest Look at What It Means to Be White* (Downers Grove: InterVarsity, 2017), 73–4.
13. Ibid., 107–8.
14. Isabel Wilkerson, *The Warmth of Other Suns: The Epic Story of America's Great Migration* (New York: Vintage, 2010).
15. Richard Rothstein, *The Color of Law: A Forgotten History of How Our Government Segregated America* (New York: Liveright, 2017).
16. Michelle Alexander, *The New Jim Crow: Mass Incarceration in the Age of Colorblindness; Tenth Anniversary Edition* (New York: New Press, 2020); cf. Chris Hayes, *A Colony in a Nation* (New York: W. W. Norton, 2017).
17. Ari Berman, *Give Us the Ballot: The Modern Struggle for Voting Rights in America* (New York: Farrar, Straus and Giroux, 2015).
18. Richard T. Hughes, *Myths America Lives By: White Supremacy and the Stories that Give Us Meaning* (2nd ed.; Chicago: University of Illinois Press, 2018), 3; idem., *Christian America and the Kingdom of God* (Chicago: University of Illinois Press, 2009).
19. Hughes, *Myths America Lives By*, 117–21.

20 Michael O. Emerson and Christian Smith, *Divided by Faith: Evangelical Religion and the Problem of Race in America* (Oxford: Oxford University Press, 2000).
21 Jim Wallis, *America's Original Sin: Racism, White Privilege and the Bridge to a New America* (Grand Rapids: Baker, 2016), 51.
22 On the political struggle to define 'Christian', see Matthew Bowman, *Christian: The Politics of a Word* (Cambridge: Harvard University Press, 2018).
23 Carol Anderson, *White Rage: The Unspoken Truth of our Racial Divide* (New York: Bloomsbury, 2016).
24 The first followed the American Civil War and the second involved the Civil Rights Movement (William J. Barber II, *The Third Reconstruction: Moral Mondays, Fusion Politics, and the Rise of a New Justice Movement* [Boston: Beacon, 2016], 97–130).
25 O Wesley Allen Jr., *Preaching in the Era of Trump* (Saint Louis, MO, Chalice, 2017), 22; cf. Michael Eric Dyson, *Tears We Cannot Stop: A Sermon to White America* (New York: St. Martin's Press, 2017), 221. See also Kelly Brown Douglas, 'Donald Trump and the "Exceptionalist" Truth about America', in Miguel A. De La Torre (ed.), *Faith and Resistance in the Age of Trump* (Maryknoll, NY: Orbis, 2017), n.p.
26 Jones, *Beyond the Messy Truth*, chap. 4.
27 Kelly Brown Douglas, 'America's Lost Soul', *Black Theology Project* (30 May 2020). Online: https://btpbase.org/americas-lost-soul/. Retrieved 23 June 2020.
28 Michelle Alexander, *The New Jim Crow: Mass Incarceration in the Age of Colorblindness; Tenth Anniversary Edition* (New York: New Press, 2020), xi. In addition to religious leaders and historians, mental health professionals have also weighed in. See Bandy X. Lee (ed.), *The Dangerous Case of Donald Trump: 27 Psychiatrists and Mental Health Experts Assess a President* (New York: St. Martin's, 2017); cf. Steven Hassan, *The Cult of Trump: A Leading Cult Expert Explains How the President Uses Mind Control* (New York: Free Press, 2019). Of course, others question the mental state of those set on opposing everything Trump (Strassel, *Resistance*). For a prescient critique of how attempts to diagnose Trump actually dehumanise Trump and his supporters (leading dehumanised supporters to seek affirmation of dignity in Trump), see Hart, *Trump and Us*, 117–40.
29 Ibram X. Kendi, *How to Be an Antiracist* (New York: One World, 2019), 9.
30 Joseph J. Ellis, *American Dialogue: The Founders and Us* (New York: Knopf, 2018), 7–8.
31 Ibid., 66.
32 On the initial reaction, see Scott Jaschik, 'Drexel Condemns Professor's Tweet' (26 Dec 2016). Online: www.insidehighered.com/news/2016/12/26/drexel-condemns-professors-tweet-about-white-genocide. Retrieved 30 Apr 2020.
33 Sheri Faye Rosendahl, *Not Your White Jesus: Following a Radical, Refugee Messiah* (Louisville: Westminster John Knox, 2018), 3.
34 Ibid., 99.
35 Ibid., 100.
36 'No presidents before Ronald Reagan had used the phrase "city on a hill" to define the very character of the American nation and its place in the world. After Reagan, virtually no serious political figure could escape the obligation to quote it' (Daniel T. Rodgers, *As a City on a Hill: The Story of America's Most Famous Lay Sermon* [Princeton: Princeton University Press, 2018], 8).

37 Sheri Faye Rosendahl, 'American Nationalism: What Are We Supposed to Be Proud of?', *Patheos* (18 July 2019). Online: www.patheos.com/blogs/sherifayerosendahl/2019/07/american-nationalism-what-are-we-supposed-to-be-proud-of/. Retrieved 9 July 2020.
38 Rosendahl, *Not Your White Jesus*, 100.
39 Cornel West, 'Introduction: To Be Human, Modern and American', in *The Cornel West Reader* (New York: Basic Civitas, 1999), xv–xx (xvii–xix).
40 Cornel West (ed.), *The Radical King* (Boston: Beacon, 2015), 74.
41 Cornel West, *Race Matters: Twenty-Fifth Anniversary Edition* (Boston: Beacon, 2017), xvii.
42 Ibid., xviii. See also his foreword to Haki R. Madhubuti and Lasana Kazembe (eds.), *Not Our President: New Directions from the Pushed Out, the Others, and the Clear Majority in Trump's Stolen America* (n.p.: Third World Press Foundation, 2017).
43 Dyson, *Tears We Cannot Stop*, 79.
44 Ibid., 77.
45 Ibid., 77–8.
46 Michael Eric Dyson, *What Truth Sounds Like: RFK, James Baldwin, and Our Unfinished Conversation about Race in America* (New York: St. Martin's, 2018), 70.
47 Ibid., 71.
48 Ibid., 7.
49 Jemar Tisby, *The Color of Compromise: The Truth About the American Church's Complicity in Racism* (Grand Rapids: Zondervan, 2019), 10.
50 Ibid., 17.
51 Ibid., 20.
52 Ibid., 15.
53 Ibid., 26.
54 Ibid., 39.
55 Ibid., 190.
56 Ibid., 185.
57 Ibid., 189.
58 Ibid., 22–3, 179–80, 202–3.
59 Ibid., 179–80.
60 Ibid., 202.
61 Charles and Rah, *Unsettling Truths*, 88.
62 Ibid., 9.
63 Ibid., 11.
64 Ibid., 205.
65 Ibid., 188.
66 Ibid., 170–2.
67 Ibid., 94.
68 Ibid., 145, 148.
69 Ibid., 193–4.
70 Ibid., 78–80.
71 Ibid., 130–1.
72 Ibid., 133.
73 Ibid., 163.
74 Ibid., 206.
75 Jonathan Walton, *Twelve Lies That Hold America Captive: And the Truth That Sets Us Free* (Downers Grove: InterVarsity, 2019), 196.

76 Ibid., 4–5.
77 Ibid., 35.
78 Ibid., 181.
79 Ibid., 98, 148.
80 Ibid., 8–11.
81 Ibid., 32.
82 Ibid., 8.
83 Ibid., 73.
84 Ibid., 169.
85 Ibid., 76.
86 Jonathan Wilson-Hartgrove, *Reconstructing the Gospel: Finding Freedom from Slaveholder Religion* (Downers Grove: InterVarsity, 2018), 17.
87 Ibid., 23.
88 Ibid., 35.
89 Ibid., 36.
90 Wilson-Hartgrove, *Revolution of Values*, 13, 70.
91 Ibid., 8.

5 Make America better

The burden of memory

I take the title for this chapter from David N. Moore: 'Whether you see America as good or something else, we should all agree that we can be better. What a shame it would be to waste our history!'[1] *Make America Better* Protestants find grounds for concern everywhere in American history. Some of them, particularly minority authors, tend to fondly remember the present (before the advent of Trump).

The *Make America Better* burden of memories resembles *Make America Lament*, but these Protestants also vocalise a deep appreciation for their deeply flawed nation. Many lament the decline of religion and morality since the 1950s. They do not, however, measure declension against a golden age. Although *Make America Better* Protestants might be partisan, they tend to lament the polarisation and ill will that are endemic to America.

Many of these Protestants think in terms of *two Americas* – one to be embraced and the other rejected. Historical analysis wrestles with the impact of past injustice on the present. The struggle is animated by ideals that are close to the heart of American history – however short-sighted or hypocritical those initially espousing the ideals were. It is patriotic to remove the plaster that previous generations placed over historical evil. Perhaps Martin Luther King Jr. and President Obama are the two foremost examples. Both spoke deeply of lament but also used the founding ideals to goad conscience-hardened whites to live up to what they professed.

Many books might fall under the heading 'Make the Church Better' – and by better, they mean more Christ-like. These books include *The Lamb's Agenda* (Samuel Rodriguez), *Onward* (Russell Moore), *The Church of Us vs. Them* (David E. Fitch), *A House United* (Allen Hilton), *How the Nations Rage* (Jonathan Leeman), *Costly Grace* (Rob Schenck), *The Immoral Majority* (Ben Howe) and *Scandalous Witness* (Lee C. Camp).[2] Many of these works take a critical view of America's history (to varying degrees), and critique the church's involvement with politics. Other books foster a historical awareness of racism and endeavour to bring about gospel-centred reconciliation (e.g. *Bloodlines* (John Piper), *Oneness Embraced* (Tony Evans), *One Blood* (John M. Perkins), *Be The Bridge* (Latasha Morrison)).[3]

The three divisions of this book, *Make America Great Again*, *Lament* and *Better* – do not overlap entirely with voting patterns. Views of history influence voting – and vice versa – but voting and views of history are not identical. This complexity is especially true of this final group.

Only a small proportion of the Protestant Right's leaders supported Trump from the outset. As noted by Frances FitzGerald in *The Evangelicals*,

> Christian right leaders with a few exceptions, such as Jerry Falwell Jr. and Robert Jeffress . . . opposed Trump. . . . Progressive evangelicals opposed Trump not only because of his libertinism but also because of his xenophobia and bigotry.[4]

Initially, Trump gave Christians few reasons to support him. His early efforts to woo evangelicals were largely ineffective.[5] The original followers – the 'court evangelicals' – formed his core evangelical support.

As many studies have demonstrated, much of Trump's 'Christian' support comes from those who rarely attend church or read the Bible. In the words of Roderick P. Hart:

> White evangelicals found themselves in the Trump camp but not always comfortably. The more often a Trump Republican went to church, for example, the less likely he or she was to embrace identitarian politics or to take populist stands. Church-going Republicans were also more racially tolerant than infrequent church-goers.[6]

After securing the nomination, most white conservatives thought they faced a binary choice. Some held their nose and supported Trump. However, they would likely recoil when co-religionists sanctify Trump, and they may not join the president on his trip down memory lane.

Others on the Protestant Right vowed to protest vote (Democratic or third party). As the historian Thomas S. Kidd details, 'A conspicuous, if small, evangelical #NeverTrump movement emerged, but that movement gained traction mostly among evangelicals who do not have much access to insider Republican circles and Fox News'.[7] Russell Moore, for example, received considerable pushback from those within his denomination – the Southern Baptist Convention. He ended a controversial article that critiqued racism as follows: 'The man on the throne in heaven is a dark-skinned, Aramaic-speaking "foreigner" who is probably not all that impressed by chants of "Make America great again"'.[8]

Never Trumpers were thin on the ground in the pews, and the movement had little political impact.[9] *Make America Great Again* Protestants now gloat over how little influence ministers who were critical of Trump had over their congregations.[10]

In addition to very reluctant Trump voters and #NeverTrump evangelicals, many *Make America Better* Protestants already felt at home in the Democratic party. Voting for Trump was never a consideration. *Make America Better* Protestants are the most diverse, both in terms of theology and politics. Although they all deeply lament injustice throughout history and see great benefit in drawing attention to it, they also harness what is best in America's past as they struggle for justice and equality.

David N. Moore

Rev. Dr David N. Moore is a Church of God in Christ pastor (Santa Barbara, California) and an adjunct professor at St. Stephen's University (New Brunswick, Canada). Brian McLaren, a leader in the emerging church movement, wrote the foreword for Moore's *Making America Great Again: Fairy Tale? Horror Story? Dream Come True?* Evangelicals, Moore has come to believe, are 'covering up America's structural racism'. This cover-up makes them 'complicit in the abuse'.[11] They fixate on confessing sin but will not confess 'the sin of accommodating Western Christian supremacy that infects Church and State'.[12]

Denial is evident throughout the nation: 'The United States has never come to terms with its foundations of stolen bodies brought to stolen land'.[13] His historical critique extends overseas, noting the often-forgotten examples of Haiti, the Philippines, Cuba, Puerto Rico and Guam. 'Throughout our country's history we have found a sense of entitlement to invade only the lands of people of color'.[14]

Moore suspects that there are 'vastly different ideas of America'.[15] Some Christians have been fed for so long on apocalyptic fear that 'they need someone to reassure them that we can be "great again"'.[16] He asks MAGA supporters: 'What year would that be?' Do they want to restore Manifest Destiny, expansion into Mexico, Reconstruction, exclusively male voting, unjust working conditions or Jim Crow?[17] The nation's sordid history makes MAGA 'a fairy tale for some and a horror story for others'.[18]

When in high school, Moore won an essay contest on the theme 'Make America Better'.[19] He returned to the topic at this critical juncture in the nation's history: 'Whether you see America as good or something else, we should all agree that we can be better. What a shame it would be to waste our history!'[20] America should be better because other nations are likely to imitate it.[21] 'If we want to make America better, we must begin, perhaps, with humility. We all will become healthier humans as we love our neighbors as ourselves'.[22]

Van Jones

Van Jones was educated at the University of Tennessee and Yale Law School. He advocates for many causes – foremost among them are criminal justice reform, income equality and environmental justice. He served temporarily as an advisor to President Obama before criticism over his controversial political activism led to his resignation. Especially since the Trump candidacy and election, he has worked to bridge the partisan divide and inject a little humility, irony and compassion into public discourse.

In *Beyond Messy Truth*, Jones writes that he 'literally had [fellow progressives] laugh in my face when I told them I was a Christian'. His politics grows directly out of his faith: 'For me, and for so many others, religious belief has provided the rationale for loving our neighbors, showing compassion to strangers, and living lives of service to people and the planet'.[23] In an interview for the *Pacific Standard*, he said:

> Even when I was a hardcore leftist with Marxist commitments I never stopped being a Christian, because it's too core to who I am, too core to my sense of what the liberation struggle is about. So I was always the one Christian in the Marxist study group.[24]

As will be shown next, Jones takes a messy approach to faith, politics and history.

The United States suffers from a 'dysfunctional "politics of accusation"' that needs to be replaced with 'a "politics of confession"'.[25] As a progressive Christian, much of the book is aimed at his fellow progressives who 'still aren't learning and consistently applying the right lessons from our 2016 defeat'.[26] Learning would require more introspection and confession. 'Progressives do pretty well embracing the historically marginalized but not so well embracing the "newly marginalized" or the "about-to-be" marginalized'.[27] Trump tapped into the frustrations of newly marginalised whites, and when progressives mocked their plight, it only made Trump a more attractive candidate.

Progressives have also marginalised religion instead of embracing it. The 'party of inclusivity' should 'start by allowing more respect and room for faith in our own ranks'.[28] Jones recognises the great harm done throughout history by religious and secular regimes. However, progressives should 'honor and embrace the positive contributions of religiously inspired people'. Shutting the door on religion 'shuts progressives off from our own history'.[29]

Jones takes a similar approach to history, arguing that Americans should critique and embrace the past.

> From the very beginning of this country, America has been two things, not one. We have our founding reality and our founding dream. And the two are not the same. Our founding reality was ugly and unequal. Nobody can deny that. . . . Now, if that's all America ever was, it would command zero allegiance from anyone. It would be impossible for a decent human being to be a patriot. . . . But that's not all America was, even at the start.[30]

Trump, he fears, appeals to the ugly and unequal side of American history. Jones argues that

> At our best, our mission [as Americans] is simple. For more than two centuries, we have been working to close the gap between the ugliness of our founding reality and the beauty of our founding dream. Each generation tries to narrow that gap a little more than the last one did.[31]

In this respect, the American mission remains the same into the Trump years, even though it seems to have taken a considerable step back.

Jim Wallis

Jim Wallis is the founder, president and editor-In-chief of *Sojourners*. Through writing, advocacy and speaking, he has long worked to apply the gospel to issues of race. He put the final touches on *America's Original Sin* shortly after the 2015 Charleston church massacre that took place just after Trump had announced his candidacy.

Wallis recounts a controversial claim from a 1987 *Sojourners* article: 'The United States of America was established as a white society, founded upon the near genocide of another race and then the enslavement of yet another'.[32] Over the decades, more Americans have come to accept this. 'Yet to speak honestly of such historical facts is to be charged with being polemical, divisive, or out of date'.[33] Historical racism must be talked about since the effects are felt everywhere. Whites are often not aware of their privilege or how implicit and explicit biases adversely influence minorities.[34]

For Wallis, America's unrivalled diversity 'is essential to our greatness' – even though it often creates conflict. This 'original racial diversity was a product of appalling human oppression based on greed'.[35] However,

America has a mission – framed in terms of the preamble to the Constitution (seeking 'a more perfect union'). American failures evidence the

> unfinished business of challenging and ending racism, an agenda that is not finished and never will be. . . . The path forward is the constant renewal of our nation's ideal of the equality of all our citizens under the law – which makes the American promise so compelling, even though it is still so far from being fulfilled. Our highest and most inspirational points as a nation have been when we have overcome our racial prejudices; our lowest and ugliest points have been when we have succumbed to them.[36]

Failure does not nullify the American experiment – it underscores the need to practice what was preached long ago.[37]

Wallis envisions a bridge that must soon be crossed – the transition to a 'majority of minorities – with no one race being in the majority'.[38] He dwells on President Obama's 2015 remarks at the 50th anniversary of the march across the Edmund Pettus Bridge in Selma. The president made statements like the following:

> [Selma was] 'a contest to determine the true meaning of America'; 'the idea of a just America and a fair America, an inclusive America, and a generous America . . . ultimately triumphed'; 'what greater form of patriotism is there than the belief that America is not yet finished'; 'it is in our power to remake this nation to more closely align with our highest ideals'; '[we must] do what we can to make America better'.[39]

Wallis, via Obama, harnesses patriotism for confession, reconciliation and reform.

Since the publication of *America's Original Sin*, Wallis has frequently reflected on race, white Christianity and Trump. In 'White Christian Complicity in Trump's Victory', he said, 'the vast majority of white evangelicals acted more white than evangelical'. He praised leaders like Russell Moore (President of the Ethics & Religious Liberty Commission for the Southern Baptist Convention) who took hard stands on racism during the election. However, it is not too late for others to confront racism:

> Repent of the sin of racism. It's time for a serious study of the history of racism in America and the narrative that must be changed. . . . Studying racism in the era of Trump will be an act of reconciliation and resistance.[40]

In *Christ in Crisis?* he called on Christians to recommit to Jesus, recognise America's unjust history and make God-honouring choices in the present:

'Easy or simplistic historical parallels are never helpful. History doesn't repeat, as many have said, but it does sometimes rhyme'.[41] He wants Christians to be more adept in discerning these rhymes across the centuries.

Eric Mason

'The Woke Church must understand its history',[42] writes Dr Eric Mason, founder and pastor of Epiphany Fellowship in Philadelphia. As a theologically conservative African American, he has long felt as if he has lived between two worlds. 'I found myself exegetically at home with my conservative family on the doctrines of grace, but ethically at home with my liberal family on issues of race and justice'.[43] Conservative Christianity 'has become more confusing', and this discomfort could be remedied if the white church 'awaken[ed] to the far-reaching effects racism continues to have'.[44] However, 'One of the most difficult things for me to deal with is the refusal for many evangelicals to acknowledge the truths about what has happened in our country'.[45]

Mason gives the church plenty to lament – culling examples from American history.[46] Of particular importance, 'Many modern mainline denominations played a role in soothing the conscience of those involved in the oppression of slavery by creating theologies and ideologies that justified these atrocities. One such ideology was that blackness was a curse'.[47] These details form part of the American church's family history, and it can be difficult for families to talk about their past. 'When America tells African Americans to forget about the past when we haven't even talked about it, that's unhealthy'.[48] History does not remain in the past. 'We must ask how this history is still affecting us today'.[49] And 'If our theology isn't wide enough to fit racial equality and fighting injustice within it, then, my friend, our theology is wanting'.[50] His hope is in Christ who transforms individuals and, through them, societies.

Mason mourned over but still embraced conservative Christianity, and his approach to history is similar. America must be held 'accountable for what it promised to do' in its founding documents.[51] He is fully aware that the founders never intended these privileges for non-whites. However,

> I believe the Declaration of Independence makes the greatest affirmative statement about reconciliation in human history. . . . America was different from the start. We were going to be a nation that reflected the divine values of God's kingdom, one nation from all nations under heaven, under God.[52]

The problem was not with the ideals; it was the weak determination to implement them.

John Fea

John Fea is Professor of American History at Messiah University in Mechanicsburg, Pennsylvania. In his history of evangelical support for Trump, he identifies three recurring themes: 'Fear. Power. Nostalgia'.[53] He argues that

> Despite the biblical passages exhorting followers of Christ to 'fear not', it is possible to write an entire history of American evangelicalism as the story of Christians who have failed to overcome fear. Evangelicals have worried about the decline of Christian civilization from the moment they arrived on American shores in the seventeenth century.[54]

Many white Christians believe America is (or was) a Christian nation. As a historian, he questioned the accuracy of these claims. As a Christian, he called the 'belief that the United States is a Christian nation . . . a form of idolatry'.[55] Fears of decline link with grasping at power.

Historical memory is essential. 'Evangelicals' propensity for nostalgia makes them susceptible to a political candidate who wants to "make America great *again*"'.[56] Talk of a golden age often reveals more about hopes and fears in the present than about what America was ever actually like.[57] Fea, in response, wants to 'replace nostalgia with history'.[58]

Throughout the book, Fea describes non-white views of history. 'African Americans have very little to be nostalgic about', and they often view recent years as the greatest.[59] Evangelicals should learn to interpret history from African Americans. Minorities have suffered from white nostalgia and fear – and a better nation still lies in the future.[60]

> When [civil rights leaders] did turn to the past, it was often an appeal to ideals such as liberty, freedom, or justice, ideals written down in our nation's sacred documents that had yet to be applied to them completely. History was a means by which they challenged white Americans to collectively come face to face with the moral contradiction at the heart of their republic.[61]

These leaders called the church and the nation to 'live up to the principles they were built on. . . . They desperately wanted to be grafted into this imperfect but hopeful story'.[62] After an honest confrontation with the past, the church and nation might look different from the now-familiar mixture of fear, power and nostalgia.

Marilynne Robinson

Marilynne Robinson is Professor Emeritus of English and Creative Writing at the Iowa Writers' Workshop (University of Iowa). In 2016, *Time* named her among 'The 100 Most Influential People' in the world. She is known for her friendship with President Obama and her novels about domestic life, most notably *Housekeeping* (1980) and *Gilead* (2004). The Pulitzer Prize-winning *Gilead*, and the sequels *Home* (2008) and *Lila* (2014), indirectly deal with race. The main character exemplifies the moderate Christian minister who did not get involved in the fight for civil rights.[63]

As a public intellectual, Robinson has delivered dozens of papers at prestigious venues across the world. Many of these talks have been collected and published. Her essays span history, politics, science, ethics, theology, aesthetics, religion and the environment. *The Death of Adam* (1998), *When I Was a Child I Read Books* (2012) and *The Givenness of Things* (2015) reflect deeply on faith and American history. 'The values of liberal Protestantism and an interpretation of the Bible that emphasizes human dignity and social justice underwrite every page of her nonfiction', writes Alex Engebretson.[64] Her most recent collection, *What Are We Doing Here?* (2018), speaks into the Trump era.

As a progressive who loves John Calvin and the Puritans, Robinson defies easy classification. She resists ideological thinking – describing it as 'thinking that by definition is not one's own'.[65] The ideologue surrenders their thinking, their rage and their interpretation of history to another.

Polarisation feeds and is fed by ideological thinking. The Left and Right hate each other with such intensity that they are unable to see similarities. Throughout *What Are We Doing Here?*, Robinson is concerned that despair about America – a pessimistic gloom indulged and nurtured by the Right and Left – has distorted history and deprived the country of any means of accounting for what went right. 'At this time the country needs to regain equilibrium and direction. It needs to recover the memory of the best it has done, and then try to do it all better'.[66]

Americans do not know the origin story behind their noblest values, highest aspirations and cherished institutions. She traces these to Puritan New England (not to the Anglican colonies of the South). Puritan New England had its backstory in England and Calvin's Geneva. In other words, much of what went right in American history is owing to people who are either ignored, mischaracterised or demonised. 'The American Puritans were the most progressive population on earth through the nineteenth century at least. They deserve notice'.[67]

In recovering the reputation of Puritanism, she does not intend to suggest 'that we could or should return to it'.[68] She is, in fact, very critical of utopian or golden-age thinking: 'Nostalgia falsifies'.[69]

> I have read too much history to have any impulse to idealize the past. Great pity and very great respect are owed to all those generations who lived and died before us, not least because they, through war and plague and famine, conferred a precious heritage on us of art, language, music, and thought. And they conferred as well a tremendous burden of festering hostilities, vicious inequalities, and outright crimes that we have had no great success in understanding or meliorating, that we have in fact compounded.[70]

Additionally, pining after 'former greatness' has been a means of civilisational undoing.[71]

She yearns for a better telling of history:

> This country is in a state of bewilderment that cries out for good history. How are we to account for liberating thoughts and movements, things that have gone well? What has been the thinking behind our great institutions? I have found little help in answering these questions. . . . Early American historiography is for the most part a toxic compound of cynicism and cliché, so false that it falsifies by implication the history of the Western world. To create a history answerable to the truth would be a gift of clarity, sanity, and purpose.[72]

The poor health of the nation mirrors anaemic views of history.

The aversion to history can mask the most egregious and long-lasting crimes. Even with considerable gaps in historical understanding, many are confident they know the past: 'it is important to remember that history that is grossly incomplete can feel coherent, sufficient, and true'. American history, she concludes, 'is substantially false, though not exceptionally so. . . . It seems to me that for the survival of our experiment to be even imaginable the country must know itself much better'.[73] Historical paradox and complexity are not to be smoothed over. For the sake of a better America, they should be embraced.

Many Americans turn away from the good in their own history, often painting their country as uniquely evil. This self-critique might seem courageous, but it is not based on truth. America's failures are not unique:

> In Adam's Fall we sinned all, the English in Ireland, Australia, the Caribbean and here, the Belgians in Congo, the Spanish in Argentina,

the Russians in Ukraine. The list is infinitely far from complete, as we all know. Its beginnings are undiscoverable. . . . If we could let ourselves have anything like a real sense of history, we would not be so continuously surprised and bewildered by its latest permutations.[74]

Historical inquiry is preparation for understanding inequality, injustice and racism in the present. She resists the totalising and dichotomising impulse in contemporary views about the past: 'human beings and their societies and histories are mingled – that is, never only to be condemned, sometimes ingratiating or admirable. Decent mutual respect depends on an awareness of this fact, that is, on good history'.[75]

Conclusion

Make America Better Protestants agree that America needs to lament, deeply. However, they directly appeal to the ideals of the American founding to argue that criticism of the past is itself patriotic. They tend to be allergic to nostalgia. They differentiate between two Americas – the reality and the ideal. The reality was unequal and unjust; the ideal laid the groundwork for equality.

The *Make America Better* position is not between the other two but beyond *Make America Lament*. They add a vocal appreciation of aspects of the past to their critiques. These authors embrace American history – the good and the bad. A better America comes after lament, but Americans should also appreciate who and what made America progressively better.

Notes

1 David N. Moore, *Making America Great Again: Fairy Tale? Horror Story? Dream Come True?* (La Vergne, TN: Crowdscribed, 2017), 97.
2 Samuel Rodriguez, *The Lamb's Agenda: Why Jesus Is Calling You to a Life of Righteousness and Justice* (Nashville: Thomas Nelson, 2013); Russell Moore, *Onward: Engaging the Culture without Losing the Gospel* (Nashville: B&H, 2015); Fitch, *The Church of Us vs. Them*; Allen Hilton, *A House United: How the Church can Save the World* (Minneapolis: Fortress, 2018); Jonathan Leeman, *How the Nations Rage: Rethinking Faith and Politics in a Divided Age* (Nashville: Thomas Nelson, 2018); Rob Schenck, *Costly Grace: An Evangelical Minister's Rediscovery of Faith, Hope, and Love* (New York: Harper, 2018); Ben Howe, *The Immoral Majority: Why Evangelicals Chose Political Power Over Christian Values* (New York: Broadside, 2019); Lee C. Camp, *Scandalous Witness: A Little Political Manifesto for Christians* (Grand Rapids: Eerdmans, 2020). See also Tremper Longman III, *The Bible and the Ballot: Using Scripture in Political Decisions* (Grand Rapids: Eerdmans, 2020).
3 John Piper, *Bloodlines: Race, Cross, and the Christian* (Wheaton, IL: Crossway, 2011); Perkins, *One Blood*; Tony Evans, *Oneness Embraced: Reconciliation,*

the Kingdom, and How We Are Stronger Together (Chicago: Moody, 2015); Morrison, *Be the Bridge*.
4 FitzGerald, *The Evangelicals*, 628; cf. Ronald J. Sider, 'Will the Evangelical Center Remain Silent in 2020?', in Sider (ed.), *The Spiritual Danger of Donald Trump*, 88–95.
5 For an account by an early supporter, see Reed, *For God and Country*. For a reluctant, then enthusiastic, convert, see the aforementioned works of Stephen E. Strang.
6 Hart, *Trump and Us*, 175; cf. Tobias Cremer, 'Defenders of the Faith: Why Right-wing Populists Are Embracing Religion', *New Statesman* (30 May 2018). Online: www.newstatesman.com/2018/05/defenders-faith-0. Retrieved 1 May 2020; Whitehead and Perry, *Taking America Back for God*.
7 Kidd, *Who Is an Evangelical?*, 148.
8 Russell Moore, 'A White Church No More', *The New York Times* (6 May 2016). Online: www.nytimes.com/2016/05/06/opinion/a-white-church-no-more.html. Retrieved 5 May 2020.
9 Kidd, *Who Is an Evangelical?*, 148.
10 Saldin, *Never Trump*, 3. For evangelical gloating, see the works of Stephen E. Strang.
11 Moore, *Making America Great Again*, 26.
12 Ibid., 46.
13 Ibid., 120.
14 Ibid., 99. See Daniel Immerwahr, *How to Hide an Empire: A History of the Greater United States* (New York: Picador, 2019).
15 Moore, *Making America Great Again*, 95.
16 Ibid., 123.
17 Ibid., 125.
18 Ibid., 138.
19 Ibid., 113.
20 Ibid., 97.
21 Ibid., 103.
22 Ibid., 114.
23 Jones, *Beyond the Messy Truth*, 29. He frequently speaks on the relationship between faith and politics (Jesse Carey, 'Van Jones on Jesus and Why Culture Needs More Empathy', *Relevant* [26 Apr 2019]. Online: https://relevantmagazine.com/current/cnns-van-jones-on-jesus-and-why-culture-needs-more-empathy/. Retrieved 24 June 2020).
24 Rubén Martínez, 'A Politics of Compassion: An Interview with Van Jones', *Pacific Standard* (1 Aug 2017). Online: https://psmag.com/magazine/van-jones-ps-interview. Retrieved 24 June 2020.
25 Jones, *Beyond the Messy Truth*, xv.
26 Ibid., 23.
27 Ibid., 25.
28 Ibid., 29.
29 Ibid., 33.
30 Ibid., 184, 186.
31 Ibid., 187.
32 Ibid., 33.
33 Ibid., 39.
34 Ibid., 86.

35 Ibid., 10.
36 Ibid.
37 He returns to a similar theme, updating it for the age of Trump, in *Christ in Crisis? Why We Need to Reclaim Jesus* (San Francisco: HarperOne, 2019), 15, 47–8, 82–5.
38 Wallis, *America's Original Sin*, 188–9.
39 Ibid., 92–3.
40 Jim Wallis, 'White Christian Complicity in Trump's Victory and Responsibility Now for Faith, Resistance, and Healing', in Miguel A. De La Torre (ed.), *Faith and Resistance in the Age of Trump* (Maryknol, NY: Orbis, 2017), n.p.
41 Wallis, *Christ in Crisis?*, 185.
42 Eric Mason, *Woke Church: An Urgent Call for Christians in America to Confront Racism and Injustice* (Chicago: Moody Publishers, 2018), 78. For another similar book, see Loritts, *Insider Outsider*.
43 Mason, *Woke Church*, 116.
44 Ibid., 116–17.
45 Ibid., 34.
46 Ibid., 98–111.
47 Ibid., 82.
48 Ibid., 96.
49 Ibid., 122.
50 Ibid., 88.
51 Ibid., 51.
52 Ibid., 192.
53 Fea, *Believe Me*, Kindle Loc. 113. For a complementary account of evangelicals and politics, see Kidd, *Who Is an Evangelical?*
54 Fea, *Believe Me*, Kindle Loc. 982–4.
55 Ibid., Kindle Loc. 2143–4.
56 Ibid., Kindle Loc. 161–2.
57 Ibid., Kindle Loc. 2096–8.
58 Ibid., Kindle Loc. 168–9.
59 Ibid., Kindle Loc. 2033–4.
60 Ibid., Kindle Loc. 2343–4.
61 Ibid., Kindle Loc. 2468–70.
62 Ibid., Kindle Loc. 2489–93.
63 See Patricia Andujo, 'Marilynne Robinson and the African American Experience', in Timothy Larsen and Keith L. Johnson (eds.), *Balm in Gilead: A Theological Dialogue with Marilynne Robinson* (Downers Grove: InterVarsity, 2019), 100–21.
64 Alex Engebretson, *Understanding Marilynne Robinson* (Columbia: University of South Carolina Press, 2017), 101.
65 Robinson, 'Preface', in *What Are We Doing Here?*, xiv.
66 Marilynne Robinson, 'Old Souls, New World' (The Ingersoll Lecture on Human Immortality, Harvard Divinity School: 27 Apr 2017), in *What Are We Doing Here?*, 273–96 (182).
67 Marilynne Robinson, 'The Sacred, the Human' (The Truman G. Madsen Lecture on Eternal Man at the Wheatley Institution at Brigham Young University: 17 Sept 2016), in *What Are We Doing Here?*, 51–68 (61).
68 Marilynne Robinson, 'Our Public Conversation: How America Talks About Itself' (The Page-Barbour Lectures at the University of Virginia: 22–26 Feb 2016), 135–82 (173).

69 Marilynne Robinson, 'A Proof, a Test, an Instruction', *The Nation* (5 Dec 2016), in *What Are We Doing Here?*, 115–26 (121).
70 Marilynne Robinson, 'Theology for This Moment' (Honorary Lecture at the University of Lund, Sweden: 26 May 2016), in *What Are We Doing Here?*, 35–50 (38).
71 Marilynne Robinson, 'Mind, Conscience, Soul' (Plenary Address at the Religious Affections in Colonial North America Conference, Huntington Library, San Marino, California: 27 Jan 2017), in *What Are We Doing Here?*, 183–204 (185–6).
72 Marilynne Robinson, 'What Is Freedom of Conscience?' (Director's Lecture at Neubauer Collegium for Culture and Society at the University of Chicago: 5 May 2016), in *What Are We Doing Here?*, 3–16 (16).
73 Robinson, 'Our Public Conversation', 138, 141.
74 Ibid., 142.
75 Ibid., 'Our Public Conversation', 144.

6 Conclusion: confessing history from George Washington to George Floyd

When Protestants hear the call to Make America Great *Again*, they want to discuss America's deep past (17th c. to mid-1950s). However, they remember and forget different things in that history.

The previous chapters argued that stories of decline are common throughout history. Trump's Make America Great *Again* fits into this bipartisan tradition. We have seen that there are two main views of who stands to benefit from Trump's great America. There is an inclusive interpretation (Make America great again *for all persons*) and an exclusive interpretation (Make America great again *for white Christian males*).

Three chapters were devoted to differing responses to Trump's final word 'Again'. Protestants of the *Make America Great Again* persuasion tend to gloss over historical injustice and focus on restoring aspects of America lost since the 1950s. *Make America Lament* Protestants do not believe America was ever great – not with its history of racism, sexism and exploitation – and they think America will be great only if it confronts national sins. These two approaches are largely incompatible – although, of course, that does not make them both wrong.

If we desire to bridge polarisation in the present, Americans need more common ground in what they remember about the past. If *Make America Great Again* Protestants have a hard time articulating what went wrong in American history, *Make America Lament* Protestants have a hard time articulating what went right.

Make America Better Protestants frame the critique of historical injustice as an act of patriotism. They may not think America was ever great, but they strive to make it better. This position is not between the two poles but beyond the *Make America Lament* position. They add to lament a tempered and qualified appreciation for the flawed figures in American history – unjust hypocrites though they be.

For all of these groups, discussing history is not merely an intellectual exercise. History barges into the present in fights about religious liberty or the role of Christianity in the public sphere. Historical injustice influences medical treatment, housing and education; it rears its ugly head in racial profiling; it surfaces in assumptions about who should be admired in American history.

Police brutality and the memory of injustice

On 25 May 2020 a white officer of the Minneapolis police department killed George Floyd, an African American who was accused of using counterfeit money. After nearly nine minutes with the officer's knee upon his neck, Floyd died. The pleas of bystanders went unheeded, as did Floyd's gasping, 'I can't breathe'. Three other police officers failed to intervene, and it was all caught on camera. Gone was the pretext of self-defence that has become commonplace in many responses to police killings.

The reaction to Floyd's death underwent three important developments. The killing was so egregious that it seemed to many, for a moment, that the country might be able to admit some sort of systemic problem with racialised policing. The killing was widely condemned as 'murder'. Protests quickly spread around the country and around the world. Even the president tweeted of 'the very sad and tragic death in Minnesota of George Floyd' – although his strong support for law enforcement in the tweet angered many (@realDonaldTrump, 27 May 2020). Many protesters feared there would be no substantive change to policing (consider the 2016 Minnesota killing of Philando Castile that resulted in a 'not guilty' verdict).

In a second development, some protests against police brutality turned into riots. The unrest initially centred on the location of Floyd's death and also on the Minneapolis 3rd Precinct, which was burned. By 1 June, an estimated 250 buildings in the Twin Cities were damaged, looted or destroyed – many of them minority-owned, small businesses along Minneapolis's vibrant and diverse Lake Street corridor.[1] By 16 June, the number was put at 700.[2]

Trump positioned himself as the defender of George Floyd's memory. He castigated 'THUGS' and those 'looting'. This tweet was widely condemned for echoing racists and glorifying violence because he warned that 'when the looting starts, the shooting starts' (@realDonaldTrump, 29 May 2020).

The destruction of property was like an inkblot test, bringing out the biases of those observing it. The president was quick to argue that rioting stemmed from greed, not grief. Because Minneapolis is known as a very progressive city, the president linked unrest with Democratic policies and blamed the violence on anarchists and Antifa. A mirroring narrative blamed right-wing provocateurs. For some, the unrest became Exhibit A in the case for law enforcement. For others, the protests brought welcomed calls for the abolition of the police.

Conclusion 79

A third development focused outrage on symbols of oppression in America's deep past. Racialised policing has its own deep history. To curb police brutality, America must confront its past. This argument was not new, but it was made with increased urgency. More Americans were saying 'black lives matter', even many who disagreed with much of what the Black Lives Matter movement stood for.[3] Now many protesters were demanding – not requesting – a reevaluation of who was deemed worthy of public commemoration. Some were unwilling to wait for symbols of oppression to be removed.

These calls were not the first major push for the removal of monuments during Trump's presidency. At the 2017 white nationalist 'Unite the Right' rally in Charlottesville – a rally that saw violence between Swastika-clad marchers opposing the removal of a Confederate statue and anti-racist counter-protesters – one anti-racist activist was murdered.

In a 15 August 2017 press conference, Trump defended his interpretation of Charlottesville. He said both groups contained violent provocateurs and 'very fine people, on both sides' – 'and I'm not talking about the neo-Nazis and the white nationalists – because they should be condemned totally'. The press latched on to his 'very fine people' comment, but the surrounding dialogue about monuments is insightful. Trump warned against the logic that would be unleashed by the removal of Confederate monuments – statues deemed by many to be too racist for public consumption.

Trump argued that the same logic that would fell Robert E. Lee would also bring down George Washington, who 'was a slave owner', as Trump pointed out. The member of the press corps responded that 'George Washington and Robert E. Lee are not the same'. Trump then pointed out that Jefferson would also fall. The member of the press corps said 'I do love Thomas Jefferson'.

Trump's George Washington and Thomas Jefferson examples seemed like a *reductio ad absurdum*. He highlighted Washington's slave ownership; the media overlooked it. He highlighted Jefferson's racism; the media overlooked it. Trump placed the press corps in a catch-22. Admire the founders and Trump makes it clear they revere white supremacist slaveholders. Denigrate the founders and risk a verbal lashing or a tweetstorm about how the press seeks to destroy history.

By the summer of 2020, the cultural ground shifted dramatically. As reported by Annie Gowen in *The Washington Post* on 7 July 2020:

> A review of news reports found at least 150 statues and memorials nationwide have been torn down by protesters or removed for safekeeping by local authorities in the aftermath of the May 25 death of George Floyd, which has sparked a historic reckoning on race and justice and has reignited debate about cultural iconography in the country.[4]

80 *Conclusion*

Although the protesters initially targeted monuments associated with the Confederacy, the iconoclasm widened. From Christopher Columbus to leaders who died in recent memory, monuments were rendered as vulnerable as the persons they oppressed. George Washington, Thomas Jefferson, Francis Scott Key, Abraham Lincoln, Ulysses S. Grant and Theodore Roosevelt have all been protested, toppled or removed. The legacies of religious figures like George Whitefield or women's rights icons like Margaret Sanger are coming under scrutiny for their white supremacy. At the time of writing, statues of colonial America have not been widely targeted. It remains to be seen if the 400th anniversary of Plymouth will push iconoclasm deeper into America's past.

The attempted arson of a church in Washington, DC, coupled with the activist Shaun King's call to remove 'white' depictions of Jesus, stoked fears. Trump said removing Jesus is 'Not gonna happen'.[5] Several Catholic churches across the country have been vandalised or burned, and religious symbols like Jesus or the Virgin Mary have been spray painted, burned or decapitated. On 11 July, a man crashed into a Catholic church in Florida during preparations for Mass. He then poured gasoline and set it on fire. The Ancient Order of the Hibernians (America's oldest and largest Irish Catholic organisation) said, 'We would remind National News editors of the Latin legal maximum "*qui tacet consentire videtu*" (*silence implies consent*); their silence on the rising tide of anti-Catholic violence is shameful'.[6] Silence = violence. Investigations are ongoing, but conservative pundits argue Black Lives Matter desecration knows no bounds.

In the 2017 dialogue cited earlier, Trump sounded paranoid for his slippery slope argument. Now many interpret his caution as prophetic. All of American history seemed too toxic to admire. There was an overlooked upside to all this controversy: Five years after Trump descended his golden escalator, announced his candidacy and animated his base with calls to Make America Great Again, he was finally pushed to articulate when America was great and who contributed to that greatness.

Donald Trump: the power of positive history

As the protests widened and riots spread to other cities, many felt that America's fundamental institutions were under attack. Family, faith and country were placed on a defensive footing. Family because Black Lives Matter also aimed to 'disrupt the Western-prescribed nuclear family structure'[7] – a statement of purpose that many on the Right interpreted as militantly anti-family. Faith, likewise, came under attack. After someone tried to burn St. John's Episcopal Church in Washington, DC, the president forcibly cleared protesters and posed for a picture in front of the church, Bible in hand. After an increasing number of statues were toppled, the president insisted on a Fourth of July celebration in front of Mount Rushmore. Trump protects the family. Trump protects Christianity. Trump protects history. Voters elected him for such a time as this.

Trump's Mount Rushmore speech (3 July 2020) was one long exposition of exceptionalism.[8] It bears some likeness to the old Puritan 'remembrancer' sermons where the minister recounted God's faithfulness in history to spur on covenant obedience. It also closely followed many of the arguments made in Eric Metaxas's *If You Can Keep It*. This speech was, perhaps, Trump's clearest articulation of the final word in Make America Great *Again*.

From the founding, through Manifest Destiny and into a future Mars landing, Americans should be proud and confident. 'Americans must never lose sight of this miraculous story', and if Americans harness the resources of history, 'the best is yet to come'. His speech was remarkable for what he included and omitted (for example, not mentioning monuments to the Confederacy).

Trump called Mount Rushmore a 'monument to the greatest Americans who have ever lived' – George Washington, Thomas Jefferson, Abraham Lincoln and Theodore Roosevelt.

> This monument will never be desecrated [applause] – these heroes will never be defaced, their legacy will never, ever be destroyed, their achievements will never be forgotten, and Mount Rushmore will stand forever as an eternal tribute to our forefathers and to our freedom [applause].

Much of the greatness of these men stems from the principles they articulated and fought for:

> Our Founders launched not only a revolution in government, but a revolution in the pursuit of justice, equality, liberty, and prosperity. No nation has done more to advance the human condition than the United States of America. And no people have done more to promote human progress than the citizens of our great nation [applause].

The founders grounded rights in God and 'set in motion the unstoppable march of freedom'.

Americans stand indebted to the heroes of the Revolution, and 'Seventeen seventy-six represented the culmination of thousands of years of western civilization'. However, millennia of progress are in peril – not because of police brutality, of which no mention is made – but because of armed bands of historical revisionists. There is 'a merciless campaign to wipe out our history, defame our heroes, erase our values, and indoctrinate our children [boo]'.

He denounces as un-American the woke 'cancel culture' that is really a 'far-left fascism that demands absolute allegiance'. Radicals seek nothing less than 'to overthrow' the past. They do not seek a 'better America' but 'the end of America'. Their agenda cannot 'have a love of America at its heart'.

The fight starts with America's children and is waged with a history book. Far-left schools indoctrinate children, teaching them

> to hate their own country. . . . [A]ll perspective is removed, every virtue is obscured, every motive is twisted, every fact is distorted, and every flaw is magnified until the history is purged and the record is disfigured beyond all recognition.

The fight is not merely over the interpretation of historical details. Nothing less than the future of justice is at stake in this war over the past:

> The radical ideology attacking our country advances under the banner of social justice. But in truth, it would demolish both justice and society. It would transform justice into an instrument of division and vengeance, and it would turn our free and inclusive society into a place of repression, domination, and exclusion.

Minorities stand to lose from historical revisionism. Radical historians destroy the resources that made progress possible: 'Our opponents would tear apart the very documents that Martin Luther King Jr. used to express his dream, and the ideas that were the foundation of the righteous movement for Civil Rights'. Radicals shred King's 'promissory note'.

As historian-in-chief, Trump tells the 'true stories of [Mount Rushmore's] great, great men'. The United States 'is the most just and exceptional nation ever to exist on Earth', and it was made so by 'Judeo-Christian principles', strong families, secure borders, the prioritisation of citizens' rights and outstanding law enforcement. Trump's America stands for 'equal justice, and equal treatment for citizens of every race, background, religion, and creed'. Trump's America advocates 'free and open debate, not speech codes and cancel culture'. Trump's America embraces 'tolerance, not prejudice'.

We have returned to the 'inclusive interpretation of MAGA' outlined in Chapter 2 – but this is barbed inclusivity. Those protesting and tearing down statues – 'bad, evil people' – are not real Americans.

The speech decries activists who do not place American heroes in their historical context. Yet Trump's speech is, in its own way, devoid of context. Most importantly, he does not situate the outrage over historical monuments in the context of police brutality. Further, his romp through the past does not dwell on the history of oppression, except to highlight abolition. In other words, America is great because it removed the knee from the slave's neck, not wicked because it knelt over the slave for centuries. Trump resurrected the Colin Kaepernick controversy by saying 'We stand tall, we stand proud, and we only kneel to Almighty God' – but no mention is made of the knee on George Floyd's neck.

On the same day as his speech, the president signed an executive order for the construction of new national monuments. 'America owes its present greatness to its past sacrifices. Because the past is always at risk of being forgotten, monuments will always be needed to honor those who came before'. Great monuments, though mute, are 'silent teachers in solid form of stone and metal. They preserve the memory of our American story and stir in us a spirit of responsibility for the chapters yet unwritten'. Yes, those memorialised have 'flaws', but

> These monuments express our noblest ideals. . . . To build a monument is to ratify our shared national project. To destroy a monument is to desecrate our common inheritance.

Of those whose monuments will be constructed, 'None will have lived perfect lives, but all will be worth honoring, remembering, and studying'.

Evangelical Trump supporters routinely overlook the president's offences by saying God uses flawed persons. Trump employed a similar argument for erecting and protecting monuments. Perhaps Trump sees his own legacy in the toppled statues (as happened to Melania Trump's statue in Slovenia).

This executive order found fault with self-proclaimed censors who took it upon themselves to regulate the public sphere.

> These statues are not ours alone, to be discarded at the whim of those inflamed by fashionable political passions; they belong to generations that have come before us and to generations yet unborn. My Administration will not abide an assault on our collective national memory.[9]

With these words, Trump drew a line in the sand, detailing the penalties for crimes against memory.

Like *Make America Great Again* Protestants, Trump's executive order admitted there were historical failures, but it extolled the greatness of America's past. There is little profit in dwelling on sins, but greatness can be restored if Americans let the past instruct the present. Americans will resemble those they revere. If they look upon what was great, they will be moved to greatness.

Al Sharpton: laying American 'greatness' to rest

The prominent Baptist minister and civil rights activist Al Sharpton delivered the eulogy for George Floyd on 5 June 2020.[10] He argued that the killing 'was not just a tragedy, it was a crime. . . . And until we know the price for black life is the same as the price for white life, we're going to keep coming back to these situations over and over again'. For as long as the system remains unchanged, the protests will continue. In the face of such injustice, Trump's appeals to American greatness sound poorly timed, trite, offensive.

Sharpton preached from Ephesians 6 on spiritual warfare. 'We are not fighting some disconnected incidents. We are fighting an institutional, systemic problem that has been allowed to permeate since we were brought to these shores and we are fighting wickedness in high places'. Killings across the country were connected, but so were injustices committed across time. Even Sharpton's surname bears the mark of slavery, constantly connecting him with history: 'That's how deep race is, that every time I write my name, I'm writing American history of what happened to my people'.

Sharpton's words were aimed at the president who was more concerned with stopping 'the protests' than stopping 'the brutality'. He called out the president's hypocrisy: 'You take rubber bullets and tear gas to clear out peaceful protestors, and then take a Bible and walk in front of a church and use a church as a prop. Wickedness in high places'. Although the powers that be have abandoned people of colour, those seeking justice have 'God on our side'.

> And the same God that brought us from chattel slavery is still on the throne. The same God that brought us from the back of the bus is still on the throne. The same God that brought us from Jim Crow is still on the throne. And if we are right, he'll fight our battle, and we'll put George's name in history.

The God of justice will reward the lowly and humble the proud.

Later in June, Sharpton directly confronted American history at a Juneteenth rally in Tulsa. The day and location were both important. Trump was going to re-launch his 2020 campaign in Tulsa after COVID-19 disruptions. The first rally was scheduled for Juneteenth (19 June) – the annual celebration of the day belated news of emancipation reached the last of the slaves. The location was important because of something that happened in Tulsa long after the official end of slavery. In 1921, angry whites massacred African Americans and destroyed over a thousand homes and laid waste to what is known as Black Wall Street. Few white conservatives knew of Juneteenth before 2020, and few knew of the massacre in Tulsa. For Trump, historical ignorance was not bliss.

Sharpton's speech surveyed American history, starting with the slave trade in which only the 'strongest' survived. He then highlighted African American involvement in the Civil War. Juneteenth should be a federal holiday because it

> represented the first day in this country that you did not have legalized slavery. . . . It ought to be a Federal holiday because it's the first day this country stepped toward living up to the model that it had announced that all men were created equal. Don't forget that most of them that wrote that owned slaves; most of them that wrote that didn't even respect their own women. . . . That's why I'm a little puzzled when I hear people walking around talking about Make America Great Again. Give me the date where America was great for everybody.

He recounted the long struggle for equality. Those protesting George Floyd's murder are the key to American greatness:

> you that are marching all over America, we're the ones that will make America great for everybody for the first time. You can't be great when you handcuff a man . . . throw him to the ground over twenty dollars . . . and you are full of such venom and hate that you keep your knee on the neck of a man who could not get up and breathe. That is not greatness. Greatness is when blacks and whites and Latinos and Asians and Original Americans hit the streets all over this country and march against police oppression.[11]

MAGA is an obstacle to greatness. It must be laid to rest. Then, perhaps, America can make its first strides towards being a great nation.

Living with historical complexity

For all of their differences, *Make America Great Again* and the *Make America Lament* Protestants share a similar approach to the past: Most tend to view American history as if it were a tapestry woven primarily of one fabric. America is great. America is lamentable.

Greatness, and the recovery of greatness, forms the warp and woof of pro-Trump narratives. The disreputable aspects of American history are occasionally woven in, but failures to live up to American ideals beautify, rather than mar, the tapestry. In other words, when *Make America Great Again* Protestants mention failures like slavery, this admission of guilt highlights American greatness because America overcame disgrace. Where sin abounded, greatness abounded even more. Justice in the present requires recognising what made America great in the past.

Dishonour forms the warp and woof of other accounts of America's past. The rare white allies are sewn into the sordid fabric. Their presence renders the rest of the fabric bleaker. In other words, even the admirable aspects of American history support the argument that American history is not admirable. America's righteous deeds are sewn into filthy rags. Justice in the present requires recognising failures and hypocrisy in the past.

Perhaps on a deeper level, the groups share a related fear. *Make America Great Again* Protestants tend to fear that criticism of the past will devolve into destruction, indiscriminately consuming the good with the bad. Many are left feeling homeless (consider the titles of Arlie Russell Hochschild's *Strangers in Their Own Land* and Robert Wuthnow's *The Left Behind*). Yes, they might agree, much in the past should be lamented. But now they lament how the country they love feels disfigured beyond recognition. Trump tapped into this anxiety and promised to do something about it.

Make America Lament Protestants have a very different fear. If they give excruciating detail about how unequal and unjust American history was and then praise some tiny aspect of that history, those they are trying to persuade will ignore the bad and embrace the sliver of goodness. They cannot cede any ground to national greatness lest this short-circuit the process of national repentance. Without lamentation, bias and inequity go unchallenged. However, I suspect that if more Americans lamented history, *Make America Lament* Protestants might be more likely to mention admirable aspects of the past.

In contrast to this, the *Make America Better* approach emphasises past injustice but also stresses that there was more to persons, institutions, documents or events. It resists the zero-sum struggle over history. The bad, and the bad exists in abundance, is truly lamentable. The good, and the good exists in abundance, is truly admirable. The good is not primarily weighed against the bad. It is doubtful if any amount of good could ever outweigh the theft of land from Native Americans or the enslavement of African Americans, for example. Ignoble aspects of the past are *set alongside* noble ones – not primarily weighed against them. America falls short of its ideals, especially when they were first articulated. But these ideals also moved the country towards justice and equality.

Make America Better Protestants fear that both sides are becoming more polarised when insisting on the total truth of their incompatible histories. On a purely practical level, there is little chance that either polarised group will persuade the majority of Americans to adopt their rendering of history. Perhaps *Make America Better* Protestants also fear that after all the American 'heroes' are rightly re-evaluated, and after all the historical documents are rightly critiqued, what planks are left from which to build national identity, unity or purpose? Will these persons and documents be so denigrated that they are of little use? *Make America Better* Protestants try to build unity around a complex and nuanced view of history. Their account of the past neither renders people historically homeless (the fear of the Right) nor does it plaster over the historical injustices that continue to influence the present (the fear of the Left).

Confessing the past, connecting the dots

Creating a shared memory will not automatically create a shared politics, but it can help foster meaningful dialogue across the divide. Two debates lay at the heart of the disagreement between *Make America Great Again* and *Make America Lament*: the relative goodness of America and the impact of the past on the present. On the relative goodness of the past, we have read dozens of incompatible verdicts. Clearly, different scales are being used. On the debate about the impact of the past on the present, there is also considerable disagreement.

Many Americans do not have overlapping accounts of what happened (confessing the past) or how those events impact the present (connecting the dots). In addition to disagreeing over historical details, many Americans want to relegate systemic injustice to the past and quarantine the past from the present.

Perhaps Americans need to become more skilled at confessing the past. Consider a *confession* of faith. These documents do not claim to create truth; they claim to bear witness to truth and call for the worshiper's assent. In the same way, Americans should confess the past. American history is inseparable from racism, the theft of land and legalised inequity. Confession simply acknowledges that these things happened.

It is also important to connect the dots. There should be an acknowledgement of the ways in which many whites benefited directly and indirectly from events and attitudes stemming from America's past, even from events before they (or their families) entered the American story. As a corollary, they should confess how minorities and women are adversely impacted by a past that continues to influence the present.

If it is difficult to confess historical injustice and connect the dots to the present, working to remedy the situation takes even more effort. As told by Susan Neiman in *Learning from the Germans: Race and the Memory of Evil*, the Germans created a word for the process of differentiating between the parts of history for which restitution should be made and the parts for which Germans might feel some pride. This long-term effort is called

Vergangenheitsaufarbeitung ('working-off-the-past'). While her book is a sustained comparison of Germany and the United States, she is the first to acknowledge difficulties in measuring (and comparing) historical evils. Her work 'is about comparative redemption, not comparative evil'.[12]

Neiman lists 'crucial facets of any successful attempt to work off a nation's criminal past'. First, she argues, 'The nation must achieve a coherent and widely accepted national narrative'.[13] Because the *Make America Great Again* and *Make America Lament* positions emphasise only parts of the story, they are unlikely to become the 'widely accepted narrative'.

What details might inform the basic contours of a shared history? Let us briefly consider some details from Plymouth to the Civil War. The Right might be uncomfortable with some parts and the Left with others.

Pilgrims and Puritans felt victimised in Europe, and they sought refuge across the Atlantic among Algonquians who were recently decimated by European diseases. Most early settlers in New England desired to act justly towards the Algonquians they met, and they considered them made in the image of God. Some Pilgrims and Puritan victims became perpetrators, particularly when they resorted to slavery and warmed up to driving Native Americans off the land.[14] Still, many of our cherished national ideals have been adopted and adapted from them.

Over time, racial hierarchies developed and were religiously sanctioned. Moving into the Revolutionary era, we must confess that the founders did not extend power to women as they legalised the subjugation of people of colour. We should also acknowledge how the documents they created were expansions of liberty and rights when compared to other polities, and the logic they unleashed helped undo many of the forms of oppression they created. The founders were wary of direct religious involvement in politics. However, they assumed that most citizens would identify as some variety of Christian and that a Christian ethic would inform civic life. We should also doubt claims to Christ-like nationhood, especially during the time when slavery and Jim Crow were legal and religiously sanctioned.

As the nation expanded, America increasingly resorted to land theft from Native Americans, and a trail of broken treaties followed. Religious rationales were invented to justify westward expansion. When we come to the Civil War, we should acknowledge that states' rights and the extension of power into the West were at the heart of the debate, but it was specifically the right to own another human. Not all Confederate soldiers benefited from slavery, and many were forced to fight. Not all Union soldiers were in favour of abolition, and most did not want racial equality. The Civil War freed slaves, but the nation did not possess the resolve to bring about equality.

In many ways, the memory gap widens after the Civil War. Again, Susan Neiman is instructive:

There are several reasons for American slowness in facing our history, and one is fairly simple: there's a hundred-year hole in it, and few white Americans are even aware of that. For most of us, the period between the 1863 Emancipation Proclamation and the 1955 Montgomery bus boycott is a vague and cloudy blur.[15]

I detailed some of what took place in this 'hundred-year hole' at the beginning of the *Make America Lament* chapter, and many argue that this century was deliberately obscured. *Make America Great Again* Protestants need to become familiar with these events. Books like *Stamped from the Beginning* (Ibram X. Kendi), *The Color of Compromise* (Jemar Tisby), *Unsettling Truths* (Mark Charles and Soong-Chan Rah) or *An Indigenous Peoples' History of the United States* (Roxanne Dunbar-Ortiz) provide a comprehensive and nuanced understanding of America's racist history from the colonial era into the present.

Because many Americans mistake being anti-slavery with being anti-racist, they grossly overestimate the levelling impact of emancipation. They do not tightly link past and present because they do not know the events that link them. White Americans need to connect the dots between emancipation and the present.

Racial disparities were not created *ex nihilo*. As Ibram X. Kendi notes, they 'are older than the life of the United States'.[16] After emancipation, every attempt (often successful) was made to reduce non-whites to second class citizens. The Civil Rights Movement only partially remedied the situation. Once again, many Americans mistook the expansion of rights with anti-racism – minimising alarming continuities between slavery, the Civil Rights Movement and the present.

The *Make America Better* position, in my estimation, is the most likely to support 'a coherent and widely accepted national narrative'. It is not a Goldilocks position that says 'America is not as bad as one side claims and not as good as claimed by the other side'. This, of course, may or may not be true – but it is not the *Make America Better* argument. Rather, *Make America Better* comes after *Make America Lament*. It does not detract from lamentation. It is a critical step beyond it. Having confessed the past, having recognised the ways the past impacts the present, having determined to work towards restitution and conciliation, what now? How does one interact with the history they lament? In what parts of history can Americans take pride?

The *Make America Better* position holds history in tension. The repulsive aspects of America's past, and they are legion and truly evil, are not all there is to the story. They may not be able to confirm that America was ever great, and certainly not for everyone. To return to David N. Moore's quote:

'Whether you see America as good or something else, we should all agree that we can be better. What a shame it would be to waste our history!'

Make America Better Protestants find in the past – in the individuals, institutions, events and documents that are riddled with hypocrisy and short-sighted exclusion – the grounds for working towards a more just and equal America.

Perhaps the greatest strength of this position is in how it frames the struggle ahead. Owning the past and rectifying wrongs is what responsible and mature nations do. Self-critique is patriotic. As Susan Neiman argued in *Learning from the Germans*, 'Having the will to face your shameful history can become a show of strength'.[17]

Notes

1. Khristopher J. Brooks, 'In Minneapolis, a Vibrant Neighborhood Now Looted, Burned and Heartbroken', *CBS News* (1 June 2020). Online: www.cbsnews.com/news/minneapolis-longfellow-neighborhood-lake-street-business-community-property-damage/. Retrieved 8 July 2020.
2. 'Minneapolis Issues Map Showing Extent of Buildings Damaged in Unrest Over George Floyd's Death', *CBS Local* (16 June 2020). Online: https://minnesota.cbslocal.com/2020/06/16/minneapolis-issues-map-showing-extent-of-buildings-damaged-in-unrest-over-george-floyds-death/. Retrieved 8 July 2020.
3. See, for example, R. Albert Mohler, Jr., 'Black Lives Matter: Affirm the Sentence, Not the Movement', *Public Discourse* (18 June 2020). Online: www.thepublicdiscourse.com/2020/06/65132/. Retrieved 8 July 2020.
4. Annie Gowen, 'As Statues of Founding Fathers Topple, Debate Rages Over Where Protesters Should Draw the Line', *The Washington Post* (7 July 2020). Online: www.washingtonpost.com/national/as-statues-of-founding-fathers-topple-debate-rages-over-where-protesters-should-draw-the-line/2020/07/07/5de7c956-bfb7-11ea-b4f6-cb39cd8940fb_story.html. Retrieved 8 July 2020.
5. Libby Cathey, 'Trump on Talk of Taking Down Statues of Lincoln, Jesus: "Not Gonna Happen"', *ABC News* (24 June 2020). Online: https://abcnews.go.com/Politics/trump-talk-taking-statues-lincoln-jesus-gonna-happen/story?id=71437172. Retrieved 16 July 2020.
6. Neil Cosgrove, 'Deafening Media Silence in Reporting of Wave of Catholic Church Attacks' (13 July 2020). Online: https://aoh.com/2020/07/13/deafening-media-silence-in-reporting-of-wave-of-catholic-church-attacks/. Retrieved 16 July 2020.
7. 'What We Believe', *Blacklivesmatter.com*. Online: https://blacklivesmatter.com/what-we-believe/. Retrieved 8 July 2020.
8. 'Remarks by President Trump at South Dakota's 2020 Mount Rushmore Fireworks Celebration at Keystone', *South Dakota* (3 July 2020). Online: www.whitehouse.gov/briefings-statements/remarks-president-trump-south-dakotas-2020-mount-rushmore-fireworks-celebration-keystone-south-dakota/. Retrieved 7 July 2020.
9. Donald J. Trump. 'Executive Order on Building and Rebuilding Monuments to American Heroes' (3 July 2020). Online: www.whitehouse.gov/presidential-actions/

executive-order-building-rebuilding-monuments-american-heroes/. Retrieved 6 July 2020.
10 'Reverend Al Sharpton Gives George Floyd Funeral Eulogy', *Rev.com*. Online: www.rev.com/blog/transcripts/reverend-al-sharpton-george-floyd-funeral-eulogy-transcript-june-9. Retrieved 8 July 2020.
11 Al Sharpton, Juneteeth Speech in Tulsa, Oklahoma (19 June 2020).
12 Neiman in *Learning from the Germans*, 32.
13 Ibid., 84.
14 See Matthew Rowley, 'Godly Violence: Military Providentialism in the Puritan Atlantic World, 1636–1676' (PhD thesis; University of Leicester, 2018), 33–59, 153–86.
15 Neiman in *Learning from the Germans*, 34.
16 Kendi, *Stamped from the Beginning*, 13.
17 Neiman in *Learning from the Germans*, 32.

Index

abortion 6, 26–7, 29, 39–40, 48, 56
Alberta, Tim 26
'all lives matter' 19
Alt-Right 21–2, 49
anarchism 78
Anderson, Kurt 4
Antifa 21, 32, 78
anti-racism: different from anti-slavery 8, 47, 89; different from civil rights 48, 89; Trump as anti-racist 18–19
Atwood, Margaret 4

Bakker, Lori 41
Barber II, William J. 49, 58
Barna, George 28
Barton, David (WallBuilders) 4, 28
Bauer, Gary 31
Bible (individuals and groups): Canaanites 55; Cyrus (Trump) 38–41; Jehu (Trump) 38; Jesus 5, 51–2, 56–7, 63–4, 68–70, 80, 88; Jezebel (Clinton) 38; Joshua 32; Moses 5; Nehemiah 40; Satan 32, 39
Bible and theology: Bible reading in public school 26–7; biblical history linked with American history 4, 32, 38–9; biblical national foundation 6, 28, 37–8; biblical values 14; Black Theology 31, 47; distorted by racism 51–62; eschatology 31, 38–41, 44n66, 49, 65; Gospel 55, 58, 64, 67; lament 46–7; Make the Church Better 63–4; as national foundation 46; patriotic bibles 28; patriotic churches 31–2; sanctifies racial hierarchy 54–5, 88; spiritual warfare 84–5; White Theology 31, 46–8

Black Lives Matter 19, 55–6, 79–80
Brooks, Arthur C. 9, 22
Brown, Austin Channing 47
Brown, Michael L. 6, 13, 37–8
Burns, Mark 19, 31
Bush, George W. 15

Cahn, Jonathan 38
Calvin, John 71
Camp, Lee C. 63
Charles, Mark 7, 14–15, 55–6, 89
Clinton, Bill 15
Clinton, Hillary: African American Protestant support for 6; as Jezebel 38; racism, charge of 15, 56
Coffey, John 4–5
critical race theory 50–1

D'Antonio, Michael 15–16
decline *see* United States trajectory (decline)
Deep State 41
Dobson, James 31
Douglas, Kelly Brown 50
Dunbar-Ortiz, Roxanne 89
Dyson, Michael Eric 7, 53–4

Eberstadt, Mary 3
economic inequality, disparity or exploitation 1–2, 28–31, 33, 39–41, 46, 48, 53, 77, 89
Ellis, Joseph J. 50
Engebretson, Alex 71
Evans, Tony 64

facism: Alt-Right and Nazis 21; America and Nazis 56, 87–8; Antifa

21, 32, 78; MAGA and Nazis 22; Trump condemns 'far-left fascism' 82; Trump condemns neo-Nazis 79; *Vergangenheitsaufarbeitung* ('working-off-the-past') 88
fake news 19
Falwell Jr., Jerry 31, 41, 64
Falwell Sr., Jerry 4
Fea, John 7, 28, 31, 70
Fetzer, Joel S. 20
Fitch, David E. 28, 63
FitzGerald, Frances 64
Floyd, George: Al Sharpton's eulogy 8, 84; Black Lives Matter 78–80; Juneteenth Rally, Tulsa (2020) 8, 84–5; killing of (2020) 7, 50, 54, 78–80; and Philando Castile, Breonna Taylor, Ahmaud Arbery 50, 78; protests and riots 78–80; Trump's Mount Rushmore speech (2020) 7, 80–3
Freedom From Religion Foundation 28

Gingrich, Newt 19
Giroux, Henry A. 46
Goeglein, Timothy S. 4
Gorski, Philip 14, 20
Guinness, Os 6, 35

Hagee, John 39–40
Hart, Drew G. I. 46
Hart, Roderick P. 17, 30, 64
Hedges, Chris 13
Hill, Daniel 48
Hilton, Allen 63
history: complex and contradictory 9, 72, 87–90; confessing 87–90; disrespecting or destroying 6, 26, 35, 78–83; empathy and critique 10; impact on the present 3, 46–91; *see also* monuments
Hochschild, Arlie Russell 10, 21, 86
Horowitz, David 19
Howe, Ben 63
Huckabee, Mike 31–2, 40
Hughes, Richard T. 49

Islam 15, 19, 32, 37

Jeffress, Robert 6, 31–2, 64
Jones, Van 7, 9, 22, 66–7

Kaepernick, Colin 83
Kendi, Ibram X. 50, 89
Kennedy, D. James 4, 28
Kidd, Thomas S. 64

law: *Abington v. Schempp* (1963) 26; activist judges 32; *Brown v. Board of Education* (1954) 48; *Burwell v. Hobby Lobby* (2014) 27; the Constitution 26–7, 34, 47, 55–7, 68–9, 90; *Engel v. Vitale* (1962) 26; Johnson Amendment (1956) 26, 31–2; *Lawrence v. Texas* (2003) 27; *Masterpiece Cakeshop, Ltd. v. Colorado Civil Rights Commission* (2018) 27; *Obergefell v. Hodges* (2015) 27; *Priests for Life v. HHS* (2012) 27; religious freedom (First Amendment) 27, 31, 77; *Roe v. Wade* (1973) 26–7, 48, 56; *Romer v. Evans* (1996) 27; Supreme Court 26–7
Lecrae 54
Leeman, Jonathan 63
Lewandowski, Corey 19
LGBTQ+ 2, 20, 27, 47
Libertarian 22
Liberty University 39
Limbaugh, David 2
Loritts, Bryan 9–10
Luther, Martin 35–7

MAGA time machine 21–2, 50
Make America Better Protestants 63–77, 86, 89–90; burden of memory 63–5; overview of 3, 6–7
Make America Christian Again 28
Make America Great Again (MAGA) (slogan) 2–3, 5, 30, 53, 64, 70, 77, 80, 85; emphasizes decline 5, 14, 77; emphasizes greatness 5, 14, 77, 82; greatest year 15; inclusive interpretation of 6, 18–19, 77, 82; exclusive interpretation of 6, 19–21, 77, 82; restores negative aspects of past 7, 50, 57–8, 65; Trump's description of 18–19
'Make America Great Again' (song by Gary Moore) 32
Make America Great Again Protestants 26–45, 77, 83, 85–8; burden of memory 6, 26–31; overview of 3, 6, 31

Make America Lament Protestants 46–62, 77, 85–8; burden of memory 7, 46–51; overview of 3, 6–7
Make America White Again 21, 49–50
Manuel, David 4
Marshall, Peter 4
Mason, Eric 7, 69
McEnany, Kayleigh 14
McLaren, Brian 65
memory: burden of 6, 26–31, 46–51, 63–5; century-long memory gap (c.1863–c.1955) 48, 88–9; divided 3, 55, 86–90; forgetting history 2, 5, 8, 32, 47, 53–4, 57–8; nostalgia 15, 20–1, 34, 36, 41, 46, 49, 52–3, 58, 63, 70–2; remembering history 2, 5, 8, 32; 'rememory' and 'disremembering' (Morrison) 53–4; shared 1, 8, 77, 88–90; Trump as defender of 80–3
Metaxas, Eric 6, 34–7, 41, 81
Miller, Arthur 4
monuments: biblical warrant for 32; erecting new 83; influence behaviour for good 32; protection of 32, 80–3; removal of 36, 79–80; targeting religious symbols 79–81
Moore, David N. 7, 63, 65–6, 89
Moore, Johnnie 31
Moore, Roy 20
Moore, Russell 63–4, 68
Morrison, Latasha 47, 64

nationalism 20–1, 35; Christian 52; civil-religious 20; and racism 20; secular 20; white 21, 79; white Christian 20–1, 56–7
Native Americans: broken treaties 88; genocide 46, 55, 57–8, 67; and immigration reform 56; injustice towards 7–8, 34, 36–7, 46, 51, 53, 55–6, 67 (*see also* racism); land theft or expulsion 7, 46, 51, 53, 55–7, 58, 65, 87–8
Neiman, Susan 87–90
New World Order 39

Obama, Barack: colour blind society, hopes of 49–50; Edmund Pettus Bridge Speech (2015) 68; *Make America Better* 63; and Tea Party 46; Trump as backlash to 50; un-American or un-Christian 49
Owens, Candace 17

patriotism: critique as patriotic 7, 63–77, 90; critique of 7; embrace of 7
Peale, Norman Vincent 14
Pence, Mike 20
Perkins, John M. 64
Pew Research Center 27–8
Picciolini, Christian 10
Piper, John 64
polarisation 1, 3, 8, 35, 63, 71, 77, 86
Poniewozik, James 15, 21–2
populism 13–14
Posner, Sarah 17, 38, 40, 89
presidential election: 2000 15; 2008 49–50; 2012 39; 2016 13–15, 18–19, 38–40, 50, 53, 66–7; 2020 2, 9, 15, 30, 32, 41, 55, 84; God's role in 27–8
progress 8, 35; backlash against 26–31, 50; creates victims 26–31; gender equality 2; racial equality 2
prophets or 'prophecy experts' 6, 38–41

racism: church complicity in 51–73, 88; conciliation 55–6; criminalization of colour 48, 58; denial of 47, 50, 53–5, 65, 69; downplaying history of 2, 28, 31–41, 83, 86–7; and immigrants 19; and Islam 19; Jim Crow 41, 48, 56, 58, 65, 84, 88; on the Left 6, 18–19, 40; lynching 35, 47–8, 56; mass incarceration (New Jim Crow) 7, 40, 50, 56–7; and minorities 6, 19–21; in the North 48; police brutality 7, 10, 49, 53, 78–85; post-emancipation denial of rights 48; on the Right 6, 40, 46–62; the Right confessing historical racism 2, 22, 28, 31–41; segregation 37, 48, 56; spiritual not political matter 58, 71; structural 47–8, 53, 65; voter suppression 7, 48, 56; white ignorance of historical racism 47–8; white privilege 29, 40, 67, 67, 69, 87; white rage 49–50; white supremacy 7, 10, 15, 17, 20, 22, 29–30, 49, 53, 57, 79–80
Rah, Soong-Chan 7, 14–15, 55–6

Reed, Ralph 17, 31
renewal *see* United States trajectory (renewal)
Republican National Convention (2016) 18–19
Robertson, Pat 4
Robinson, Marilynne 4, 7, 71–3
Rodriguez, Samuel 63
Rosendahl, Sheri Faye 7, 51–2

Sanders, Bernie 13, 22
Schenck, Rob 63
Scott, Darrell 18
secularism: conflict with religion 21, 26–32, 66; harmful forms of 3, 20, 66; secularised puritanism 4
Sharpton, Al 7, 84–5
Soper, J. Christopher 20
Stewart, Katherine 46
Strang, Stephen E. 17, 40–1

Taylor, Mark 39–40
Thomas, Cal 6, 32–3
Thompson, Derek 5
Tisby, Jemar 7, 54–5, 89
Toma, Danny 26
Trump, Donald J.: accomplishments 17; affinity for authoritarian leaders 19; defends Christianity and Bible 27, 80–1, 84; description of American greatness 16–19, 80–3; emotion, use of 30; and George Floyd 7–8, 78–83; inclusivity 18–19, 82; as instrument of God 27–8, 38–41; Israel, support for 32, 39; offensive 16, 19–21, 30; as opposed to God 84–5; polarising figure 5; political correctness 37, 40, 49, 83; racism, charge of 15, 17, 55–6; sexism, charge of 15, 20 (*see also* women); Twitter 16–17, 20, 78–9; view of African Americans 16–17; view of history 16
Trump, Donald J. (writings and speeches): *The America We Deserve* (2000) 16; *The Art of the Deal* (1987) 16; *Crippled America: How to Make America Great Again* (2015) 14, 18, 27; 'Evangelicals for Trump' rally (2020) 17, 27; 'Inaugural Address' (2017) 18; 'Mount Rushmore speech' (2020) 7–8; 'New Deal for African Americans' speech (2016) 18; 'Presidential Announcement Speech' (2015) 19; 'Remarks for National African American History Month' (2019) 16–17; 'State of the Union Address' (2018) 18
Trump, Melania 83
Trump opponents: African American Protestants 6; drive people to Trump 30, 66; MAGA haters 6; #NeverTrump evangelicals 5, 64–5
Trump supporters: acknowledge flaws 17, 38, 83; anti-elitism 14, 29–30, 41; Bible, rarely read 64; dehumanisation of 22, 51; diversity of 17–19, 40; evangelical support 5–6, 13, 17, 38; and fear 13, 65, 70, 86–7; racism, charge of 29–30; value a protector 27, 38, 80–3; value emotion 30; as victims 26–31

United States (groups): founding fathers 6, 28, 39, 54, 79–83, 88; Ku Klux Klan 48, 58 (*see also* lynching); neo-Puritans 3; Pilgrims 2, 5, 13, 26, 32–3, 40–1, 88; Puritans 4–5, 8, 13, 26, 33–4, 40–1, 51–2, 71–2
United States (history): African American, injustice towards (*see* racism); Charlottesville 'Unite the Right' rally (2017) 79; Civil Rights Movement 26, 48, 52–3, 58, 63, 70–1, 82, 84, 89; Civil War 8, 32, 40, 48, 58, 79–81, 84–5, 88–9; colonial era 2–4, 37; culture wars 14, 26–31; Declaration of Independence 2, 69; Doctrine of Discovery 55; emancipation or abolition 8, 40, 47, 83–4, 88–9; Emanuel AME Church massacre (2015) 49–50, 67; founding reality *v.* founding ideal 7, 34, 64–76; Manifest Destiny 34, 53, 65, 81; minorities, injustice towards (*see* racism); Moral Majority 4; Reconstruction 58, 65; Revolutionary era 2, 6, 20, 37, 40, 81, 88; Salem witch trials 3–4;

slavery 3, 7–8, 18, 34, 36–7, 40–1, 46–8, 53–4, 58, 67, 69, 79, 83–9; Tulsa race massacre (1921) 84–5

United States (identity): American exceptionalism 4, 15, 34–5, 37, 55–6, 81–2; Christian founding (colonial or republic) 4, 6, 28, 34, 37–41, 82; Christian nation 4, 28, 49, 88; covenanted nation 4, 13, 33–4, 49, 81; ideals 6–8, 38, 49, 52, 57, 63, 68–71, 73, 81, 83–8; innocent nation 49; origin stories 5; Promised Land 19, 51, 55

United States (individuals): Adams, John 32; Columbus, Christopher 33, 57, 80; Douglass, Frederick 47; Edwards, Jonathan 57; Grant, Ulysses S. 80; Jefferson, Thomas 8, 79–83; King Jr., Martin Luther 26, 40, 52–3, 63, 82; Lee, Robert E. 79; Lincoln, Abraham 8, 26, 32, 36, 47, 56, 80–3; Neal, Daniel 1; Reagan, Ronald 18, 26, 39; Roosevelt, Theodore 80–3; Sanger, Margaret 8, 40, 80; Tillam, Thomas 13; Washington, George 8, 26, 32–3, 35, 79–83; Whitefield, George 36–7, 80; Winthrop, John 4, 51–2, 55, 57, 60n36

United States (morality): global force for good 2, 19, 35–7, 39, 81; global mixed or negative record 52–3, 65; national guilt 2, 6; national progress 2, 7–8, 73, 88; national repentance 7, 28, 58, 86; national sickness 9–10; weighing greatness or guilt 8–9, 37, 41, 86

United States trajectory (decline): from 1950s and 1960s 6, 13, 15, 21, 26–7, 33, 37, 41, 47, 63, 77; of Christian influence 2, 6, 26–45; cultural 13; 'Jeremiad' 13; moral 2, 26–45, 47; national 14, 28, 70–1; national sickness 9–10; of religious adherence 2; of white population 50–1, 68; of white Protestant population 27

United States trajectory (renewal): national progress 2, 7–8, 73, 88; renewal 2, 4, 6, 13, 18, 27–8, 30–4, 38, 41, 68, 83; renewal of covenant 4, 13, 33–4, 81

Van Engen, Abram 5
victimisation and persecution: Left as perpetrator 13–14, 26–31; persecution denial 29; Right as perpetrator 14; victims becoming perpetrators 13–14, 88

Waldman, Steven 27
Wallis, Jim 7, 67–9
Wallnau, Lance 39–40
Walton, Jonathan 7
West, Cornel 7, 52–3
West, Kanye 17
White-Cain, Paula 17, 31
white genocide 21, 50
Wilson-Hartgrove, Jonathan 7, 14
woke: criticism of 3–5, 82; Great Awakening 3–5; woke church 69
women: #MeToo 4; sexism, confessing historical 4, 8, 18, 20, 34, 40–1, 46, 53–4, 56–8, 77, 85, 87–8; sexism, downplaying historical 7–8, 28, 31, 33, 37, 39, 40–1
Wuthnow, Robert 86